HEALED AM I

Healed Am I

Overcoming the Trauma of Abuse

BEVERLY TIPTON HAMMOND

Berries On the Vine, LLC

Publication Rights

HEALED AM I: Overcoming the Trauma of Abuse

By Beverly Tipton Hammond
Copyright, 2018 by author, Beverly Tipton Hammond
Printed in the United States of America
ISBN 9780578607030 (sc)
ISBN 9780578607023 (ebook)

Bible quotations:

Scripture taken from the *New King James Version*. Copyright, 1982 by Thomas Nelson, Inc. Used by permission. All rights reserved.

Scripture taken from the *Amplified Bible*, (Classic Edition) Copyright,1954, 1958, 1962, 1964, 1965, 1987 by The Lockman Foundation. Used by permission.

Scripture quotations marked (NIV) are taken from the *Holy Bible, New International Version*, NIV, Copyright, 1973, 1978, 1984, 2011 by Biblica, Inc. Used by permission of Zondervan. All rights reserved worldwide. The NIV and New International Version are trademarks registered in the United States Patent and Trademark Office by Biblica, Inc.

Cover Photo by Brett Dorrian Benedict
brettdorian.com

Printing & Distribution: IngramSpark
www.ingramspark.com

Editor/Consultant
Royalene Doyle
Doyle Writing Services
doylewrites@comcast.net
www.doylewritingservices.com

Dedication

Every word, every page, every tear shed in the past
and during the writing of this book
is dedicated to all the men, women, boys and girls
who have experienced abuse of any kind
(physical, mental, emotional)
and especially to those who have remained silent.
To my LORD and Savior, Jesus Christ,
The Healer of my mind, spirit, emotions,
Who gave me victory over abuse and restored beauty in my
life.
And to my husband Drew, family and dear friends
who pray for me, encourage me, and support me
in my daily journey with God.

Forward by Apostle Linda Harvey

"Healing takes courage, and we all have courage, even if we have to dig a little to find it" Tori Ames

The first step of healing is recognizing that there's a wound. ***Our past is a symphony of sounds and imageries.*** Creative thoughts, expressive verbiage and seasons of laughter that echo in the archives of our mind. Each memory a collage of information that decorates or stains our soul. Reflections of past experiences may cause us to laugh out loud, replaying events that impacted our lives. Those are the days I hold onto; the sunny, lemonade, dressed in eyelet lace skirt days. A time of innocence, fun and freedom.

Some memories – the dark imprints, remain lodged in our souls. These are the tormentors. The ghosts that haunt us afresh. The cycles that cause us to scream! It was this pit of shame that stained my soul; the lair where the monsters dwelled. I carried the scars of sexual trauma; owned it and wore it like a fur that I stroked on occasion. I became the master of disguises and brilliant orator sharing lies of happiness with tear filled eyes. Eventually, I realized I had to get my life back, my real life, so I did. I took off the cloak and put on a garment of praise trusting God for my healing. Daily I would thank God for my victory and as I thanked Him, I grew stronger.

As a survivor, I understood the ripples of anguish and the bankrupt, impoverished, exhausted life. I did everything in my power to hide my brokenness; but it still oozed out. We all have something chasing us. Some hideous beast that ploughs over our lives until we are consumed and silenced. My friend, until we face the monster of sexual trauma, we will run, hide and mask ourselves. It's time to stop running and seek God for complete healing!

I met the author Beverly Hammond several years ago and discovered we had a similar testimony. I was privileged to read the draft of this book; the one you now hold in your hands. I was blessed, inspired and encouraged by the transparency of her testimony. I salute her bravery and stance that every victim will see themselves in their original state – victorious in Christ Jesus!

I give you permission to deactivate the years of trauma and ghosts that have plagued your life!

My friend, you hold the key to your deliverance! I pray that as you read this book, you will allow God to strip away the years of suffering. It's time to live! It's time to be strong and free! I believe with all of my heart, this book, *Healed Am I - Overcoming the Trauma of Abuse,* will bless and guide you onto a clear path of healing and wholeness.

Apostle Linda Johnson-Harvey
Visionary, Founder and Overseer
Fragrance of Faith Ministry, Incorporated
"Serving the Community with the Love of Christ"

Preface

**"Healed Am I" is my declaration of freedom from the
trauma of abuse!**

This book was birthed out of my personal experience; the
heartbreaking and spirit-breaking torment that came from abuse
which led me on a journey I never asked for or wanted. Yet, today,
I am able to praise God in the victory over those events and the
rebuilding of the person I am now.

The Lord has revealed to me His desire and burden to see all
His people healed and delivered from every bit of the grief and
pain we have suffered. He has led me to write these pages as a
useful tool for the healing process He gives us and a guide to freedom, especially for the ones locked in their internal, silent prison.

I remained silent until I was in my thirties. While these pages
reveal my story, they also hold much of what I've learned in over
25 years of counseling with other abuse victims who released
their past, their tormented life stories and walked toward healing.

One of the main concepts I deal with is the *internal bleeding*
we've suffered. This term describes the emotional and mental
damage—and the spiritual damage—that goes unnoticed on the
inside of each of us who have been so terribly wounded and devastated!

When the concept of *internal bleeding* came to me, I went to
Webster's Dictionary to confirm my understanding. *INTERNAL* is
a descriptive word meaning "coming from or existing on the inside. It also means "existing within the mind." Synonyms noted
are *innermost, middle* and *interior.* These definitions helped me
understand the deeper, spiritual perspective that our *internal suf-*

fering becomes buried in the *core*, the innermost part of our humanity.

The definition of the word *bleed* is "to lose or release blood because of a cut or injury." This struck me so profoundly, as all *life* is in the blood! If we were to bleed continuously we would ultimately die. The purpose of our healing process is, first, to get the "bleeding to stop."

Placing these definitions together, I came to the revelation that any type of abuse can cause us to lose the *life-giving source* that flows from the very core of our being and existence. Then I understood the parallel Truth, seen in the redemption of Jesus' shed Blood for us. His blood flowed out of Him covering the sins of all mankind. **That includes the sins of abuse committed against us.** Without the shedding of His blood we would have no forgiveness, or release from the effects of sin, as He was the perfect sacrifice for it all. His blood forever flows for us to heal and restore us! His victory over our *internal bleeding* is available to us every minute of every day!

It is my prayer for you this day that you will walk with Him in victory, too.

Respectfully walking in His service,

Beverly Tipton Hammond

Table of Contents

Chapter 1

Beginning the Healing Process

It is amazing to me how long we humans can hold in and bury our pain. I was sexually, mentally and emotionally abused between the ages of 6 and 8 years old and again in my teenage years, yet, I did not tell my parents until I was in my mid-thirties. I gave my life to Jesus Christ at the age of 14 which I believe is the reason I am still here today. I needed His Saving Grace and Mercy to supply me with His Strength so that I could endure and survive the trials and pain I would face.

I survived, but I was definitely not living my life to the fullest. I was damaged on the inside, bruised and broken with no resolution or repair for my trauma. I had worked through some elements of forgiveness and started to allow the Lord "in" to heal me and remove the roots and fruit (reactions) of those experiences. However, releasing the truth about what had happened to me (even to God) brought back painful memories, but it was liberating for me. And, of course, it was also painful for my family.

Why did I not share my abuse with anyone, especially when I was in my teenage years? I believe I was conditioned to keep quiet and that silence then became my private prison. My abuser was a family member whom I loved, which made it even harder to tell family and friends what he had done.

Strangely enough, when an abuser is someone we love, we keep the secret because we don't want to disrupt our family. I'm now aware that, as a child, I was so traumatized by my experience that I literally could not *speak* of it. I vaguely remember trying to tell another family member what was happening to me and even as the words themselves seemed to choke me, that person "hushed" me. So, in silence I remained.

Silence kills is the conclusion I've reached from these personal experiences. And today, from my association with so many precious people who have also suffered the wounds of abuse, I can make that statement as fact. **Silence kills the abused over and over again**. If we can't talk about our pain, we remain confined inside our personal prison. This, in turn, causes us further damage and negatively impacts the lives of others we know and love!

The Scripture says in Psalm 18:6
"In my distress I cried out to the Lord; I cried to my God for help.
From His temple He heard my voice; my cry came before Him into His ears."

Our damaged bodies and spirits create crutches that *seem* to support us through daily life. However, within our hearts we are *crying* in desperation, looking for help. This was true for me until I came upon a transforming moment that changed everything. To this very day I still remember exactly where I was when that moment arrived for me, effecting my life and everyone in it; when the *silence* I'd kept for years, even after another assault happened while I was in college, I was confronted by God's Grace.

I was a young minister at a Christian Church that recognized my desire to reach out to hurting people and they nurtured me with prayer and teaching. One weekend our pastors and church staff went on a retreat into beautiful, forested mountains, and I went along.

We were all in need of some personal time away to be with the Lord and to allow Him to strengthen our fellowship with each other in Him. One day after morning prayer and breakfast, I went for a walk on a hiking trail to be completely alone with the Lord. On the path, a higher hill caught my attention. I felt compelled to climb to the top. As I drew closer to the pinnacle, I *knew* the Lord was present. I also experienced a deep need to pour my heart out to my heavenly Father—specifically the anguish I was feeling from the devastating rape experience in college seven years earlier.

With tears filling my eyes, I fell to my knees, a sharp rock scraping my ankle. "God, I was raped," I shouted. "Oh, God. I was raped."

Once those words were released out of my mouth, God took all those awful moments and all the following years of pain and carried them away. I felt exhausted and elated—shocked and amazed—and full of peace (yes, the Peace that surpasses all understanding).

With my acknowledgment and willingness to speak the truth to God—to yank open the hole of silence that caused my personal *internal bleeding*—He stopped the *bleeding*! In that very moment, God showed me exactly what His Son, Jesus, had done for me on the Cross. In that very moment, He took away every wound and totally healed my heart and spirit. I felt His Peace, comfort and restoration engulf me like a warm over-sized protective blanket and I remained there with Him for quite some time.

As I descended the hill, I realized I was leaving all my pain and my past on that mountain at the very feet of Jesus Christ, the Son of the Living God! I had cried out to Him, breaking my silence and seeking freedom. God heard me and healed me! He set me completely free!

I came down that hill a new woman; a free woman; liberated by the Power and Presence of God! From that very moment I knew I was cocooned in His Love and the assurance of His complete healing. Now in my fifties, I carry the passion of this testimony as I acknowledge the healed scars and the delivering, restoring power of God through Jesus Christ!

Jesus has totally set me free from all the experiences that should have destroyed me. I not only survived, but now walk in true freedom from all past abuses! And I must say again, that I want to see every victim of abuse around the world become pain free and at peace!

> *"Then the woman, knowing what had happened to her,*
> *came and fell at His feet and, trembling with fear,*
> *told Him the whole truth.*
> *He said to her, "Daughter, your faith has healed you.*
> *Go in peace and be freed from your suffering."*
> Mark 5:33-34

When we watch the TV news, we see that time and time again people are committing suicide or senseless, brutal murders. Later we learn that their actions were part of a spiraling decent caused by broken lives, broken beliefs, and daily frustrations that destroyed them quietly and privately until they could not bear up under the pressure. This *internal bleeding*—the festering, invisible, pain that we bury deep inside of us—is why those who desperately need healing go on being *sick* for years. The true source of what is going on inside the soul is never acknowledged and they become more and more deceived into believing that taking their own life, or someone else's life, is the only way to escape their pain. They were *bleeding internally* for years and never found a way out of their mental and emotional prison.

Whether we want to believe it or not, there exists forces of evil that plague and torment us in our minds and emotions. Misdirection's, misunderstandings, twisted words and outright lies are the deceptive tools of this enemy whose warped jealously attacks all human beings.

Those who have been mentally, emotionally, physically or sexually abused, are especially susceptible and fall prey to these deceptions believing that "stuffing their pain" or *denying* it (for 5, 10, 30 years or more) keeps them safe from further harm. Thus, they remain stuck in a state of bitterness, inner turmoil and depression—alone, and in silence.

But God is real and so is the Light of God that always dispels darkness. The Light of Jesus Christ is the Spirit of God Who brings redeeming insights to our dark places, to heal, restore and revive what was once dead. It is glorious and indescribable! When we are exposed to His Light and Love, we are forever changed!

We also face another obstacle because the world we live in offers us "human resources" that too often bandage our pain but does not provide a lasting remedy or cure that will actually stop the constant flow of this unrelenting pain. Please don't misunderstand me. I believe that God uses many people to guide us to Himself and His Healing, and these include secular counselors, social workers, and medical doctors who may prescribe a specific medication. If this is where you're finding help today, I applaud you for seeking that help.

However, while these solutions can support us temporarily as we deal with our feelings, many people remain stuck or buried in the place of their deepest wounds. It is time for everyone to find the way out!!! And this is why I'm sharing the story of my life, and the collective journey of many of the amazing people I've counseled. We stand firmly to declare that the only true remedy that will stop the *internal bleeding* and pain of abuse is Jesus, God's only Son – our Redeemer, Healer and the Living Word of God.

Isaiah 53:4,5 (NIV) says,

Surely, He took up our pain
and bore our suffering,
yet we considered Him punished by God,
stricken by Him, and afflicted.
But he was pierced for our transgressions,
He was crushed for our iniquities;
the punishment that brought us peace was on him,
and by his wounds we are healed.

This is the Word of God that never returns void.

<u>What does this mean for us personally? It means that about 700 years before the human presence of Jesus, Isaiah was inspired by God to write those words. It means that today, those words still inform all of us of the Perfect Gift of Jesus Who took upon Himself the sins of all mankind and gave His life for us. It means that we have ancient verification that Jesus paid the *price* for our inequities—every wicked thing of the world—giving us personal peace, health and wholeness! All we need to do is accept His Gift, freely offered.</u>

There is no doubt that the anguish we feel is real, like suffocating on the inside and we can't breathe. We wake up in the middle of night having had a tormenting dream or simply feel numb and just can't sleep hardly at all! We believe that we're just existing from day to day; walking through the motions of rote-living, hidden from the world by various masks we wear. We think we're protecting others from the *real* person we believe we are, the bitter, broken, hate-filled *thing* that was discarded and left for dead as the result of the trauma of abuse. This aftermath can be likened to the scene of a tornado or tsunami that has come through a neighborhood and destroyed everything in its path; only the aftershocks of hidden pain and anguish remain.

But I am alive and well today to tell you that the renewing remedy comes to us directly from our Creator, the Living God, Who gave us a Promise in His Word that He would restore unto us what the enemy has stolen from us; innocence, health, peace and safety.

However, a person must surrender to God, through Jesus Christ, to find this true freedom. After being enclosed in darkness for many years, light can be uncomfortable, strange and yet so wonderfully welcoming. I encourage you to pray the following prayer out loud. It will move you forward towards your healing.

Prayer for Healing and Freedom

Dear God, I want to be totally free from all of the pain and damage done to my mind, body, soul and spirit. My heart is broken, and I find it difficult to get through the day. I believe that You can heal me from all the devastation in my heart. I ask You to set me free as I give it all to You. Let Your love heal me now; in Jesus Name, Amen!

~ ~ ~

A confirming Scripture to recall throughout your healing ~ throughout your life.

In the beginning was the Word, and the Word was with God,
and the Word was God.
He was in the beginning with God.
All things were made through Him,
and without Him nothing was made that was made.
In Him was life, and the life was the light of men.
And the light shines in the darkness, and the darkness did not comprehend it.
John 1:1-5, NKJV

Chapter 2

Shattered Pieces

"I often feel like a broken man," my friend once told me. "Like I'm broken into pieces that are only being held together by God's glory."

I sensed that there was a lot of devastation and pain in his life, yet the power and presence of God was keeping him alive. Although I personally understand that there is a price to pay for being used by God—allowing Him to use our skills, talents, physical strength—I wondered if this particular individual had to live out his life battling depression and sadness. The deceptive spirit of rejection was working full-time to keep this man in turmoil because he had been adopted and continued to feel abandoned by his birth parents. This is not God's perfect will for his life—or anyone's life. God takes the pieces of a broken life, puts them back together and restores us. However, we must give Him permission to do so.

"The thief does not come except to steal, and to kill, and
to destroy.
I have come that they may have life,
and that they may have it more abundantly.
I am the good shepherd.
The good shepherd gives His life for the sheep."

John 10:10-11, NKJV

Who is "the thief? Our enemy? It is Satan himself, the father of lies, who has been the enemy of God and His people since before earth was created. His goal is to fill us with roots of depression, anger, perversion, addiction, suicide, fear and hatred and the list goes on. Unless removed from our lives there is no real freedom. The enemy must be defeated in the spiritual realm.

I thank God for the insight He has given me in this area. Unmasking Satan has been (and continues to be) a major step in the healing process; and pulling the covers (disguises) off this culprit helps us all live the healthy and wholesome life that God has provided for us.

This enemy has isolated too many people because we were never able to truly express how we really feel to anyone, anywhere, at any time. Either no one had the patience (or courage) to listen to us or we never found the strength to share what was eating us up inside. Our words—our pleas for help—were lost in time and space and our *silence* about the abuse we'd experienced became worse than a concrete or barbed wire prison!

Satan, has a big, evil agenda that Jesus clearly revealed to us. The Apostle, John, quoted His words, *"The thief comes only to kill, and steal, and destroy"* (John 10:10a). But we now know that God sent His Son that we might have **life** and that throughout our lives that *life* grows more abundantly! He offers us a life of peace, joy and rest even in the difficult times of life. God is a refuge, comforter, and friend who brings peace in the midst of storms. He Loves us and His is the Love that heals. Jesus said:

"I have come that they may have life, and have it to the full.
I am the good shepherd. The good shepherd lays down his
life for the sheep."
John 10:10b-11 (NIV)

~ ~ ~

When a crystal glass is broken, or window is shattered, we replace or repair it because the damage done makes it inoperable and unusable. The glass can no longer hold water. The window can no longer keep out the cold. These objects therefore can no longer carry out the function for which they were designed. It was the same for me, in my life, and for my friend who expressed how *broken* he felt. It is also the same with all human beings. When we experience an act or event that shatters and breaks us, we can no longer function normally because of the trauma and the shattering that takes place within dramatically weakens our role (calling or vocation) in life. This is, indeed, a crime against our very lives and against God. Yet it pleases our enemy.

The foremost truth of the matter is that any form of shattering abuse – misuse and mistreatment of another human being – is most grievous to the individual and those around him/her. There are literally millions of muted victims around the world who have never spoken about their abuse and the devastating aftermath. Proverbs 18:14 tells us, *"A man's spirit will endure sickness, but a broken spirit who can bear?"* Until a wounded spirit is healed and restored, a slow, painful death takes place on the inside.

So how do we repair our *shattered pieces*? Those of us who have been abused instinctively mastered the creation of a self-defense system that camouflages the signs of abuse beneath layers of suppressed memories. We don't want to remember these things let alone discuss them with anyone. If we happen to recall an incident (flashback), we do our very best to wrestle it back into the forgotten files and move on with our lives. Yet deep inside, we really want to find freedom and peace. Where is that freedom? How can we discover that peace?

After years of being silent myself, I can confirm that the first step towards freedom from this painful burden is to open your mouth and tell someone that you are in fact, hurting on the inside because you were abused. On one level it is terribly difficult to accomplish. Yet, once accomplished, it seems the simplest of things to do!

A verbal release of the truth is the opening of a door in our minds, souls and spirit giving us a way to purge and heal the private pain we've been living with for months or even a lifetime. Through that process, what has been buried in our hearts is revealed and we uncover the hidden truths that have caused us to decay on the inside.

Just a quiet, whispered conversation with God, Who is always listening, will open that door.

"I was abused and I want to be free from my pain."

These words are a powerful first step towards freedom.

Even the thought of opening that door may fill you with fear, so think about it as if you're going to your primary care doctor because of unexplained physical pain; aching that radiates throughout your body. First the doctor will ask you to describe the pain; sharp, burning, intense and then ask you to give it a number from 1 (minor) to 10 (excruciating). The symptoms you describe, and the severity of discomfort will direct the doctors search for the root problem and the remedy. The goal is always to find out what is actually causing the pain and then begin treatment, leading healing and restoration to a full and active life. This same method is also part of the first steps toward receiving spiritual and emotional healing.

As the Lord's healing began to peel away the years of suffering I'd endured, I began to learn more about how to help others—being restored to the role (the calling) in my life. One of the first things that became clearer for me was understanding the definition of the word, *trauma*. I discovered that in the original Greek it means "wound," which was used to describe physical injuries. However, today we've come to understand deeper levels of this concept, including the emotional wounds that cause deep traumatic, psychological injuries.

Medical doctors, psychologists, chaplains and counselors refer to this as PTSD—a reaction to emotional trauma that usually occurs after an extremely stressful event, such as natural disasters, military combat or physical (mental or emotional) abuse. Some of the symptoms include anxiety, depression, distressing flashbacks, and recurring nightmares. Left untreated, the damage creates substantial and lasting injury to the psychological development of the individual.

Thinking of many of my friends and clients, I've known Christians and non-Christians alike, men, women, children and teens, to suffer from this PTSD emotional pain and the destructive effects. Several symptoms include sleepless nights, nightmares, depression, stress disorders, alcoholism and the repeating cycle of abusing others. This has led me to prayerfully ask God why some Christians continue to live with emotional trauma, even though the power and light of Christ lives inside of them? Many are actively engaged in efforts to reach out to heal others when, in fact, they are bleeding on the inside themselves.

Over time, His answer became clear. It is because these wounded Christians choose to overlook (deny) the root of hurt in their own soul; some may not be consciously aware that the *bleeding* wound is even there—buried in old memories. And, some may have gathered their *shattered pieces* and hidden them behind their ministries.

These precious people find it extremely difficult to open up and be honest with themselves, even as anxiety and flashbacks cause them pain. Some may acknowledge that they have bad dreams about "something bad that happened to them," yet believe if it is buried deep enough and long enough it will just go away. The truth is that it does not go away on its own. Whatever is planted in the soil of our souls is going to grow and bring forth fruit, whether good or bad.

~ ~ ~

Just the other day, when I was working in the yard, I saw an amazing example of what had found its way into the soil. It was time to clear weeds and old mulch in preparation to spruce up the front yard. The shrubs were also in need of trimming. Unfortunately, the year before, we did not clear the weeds, so much was now overgrown. What I discovered was quite a challenge, as roots from a flowering shrub had also surfaced and were entangling other bushes, hindering their growth. Roots of all kinds were crossing each other and killing other things around it. I had to cut out more roots than I wanted to in order to find their origin and then do my best to pull them completely out of the ground! Get the picture?

The roots of abuse, and the associated trauma and pain that have plagued our souls (whether we've been aware of it, or not), have been growing and strengthening, wrapping themselves around the good things and killing what we want to grow and thrive. Worse yet, our roots may also be endangering other people because of our reactions to the pain, especially when we cannot find (or consciously reveal) the root and pull it out.

This is part of the picture of deliverance, as we find our way to Jesus and accept His life, death and resurrection which brings freedom from the invading roots of bondage. Our full recovery and restoration from any, and all, personal devastation is in the Word of God. The promises given by God to His people can and will bring us back to life! For the Word of God brings life to everything it touches!

I declare to you, that at this very moment as you are reading these pages, the Spirit of the living God is moving on your heart and preparing you to be set free from all bondage and pain that you carry as a result traumatic experiences during your lifetime. How do I know this? I know because I have prayed for everyone who would read this book and believe that you will experience liberation and peace as you make this journey.

Today you have received great news! God is listening, and He is ready to give you the peace and joy that you have longed for; a life filled with abundant beauty.

~ ~ ~

I was in a church service one morning and saw God move in such an incredible way, as people came forth in that safe place and began to speak openly about their abuse experience. The more they shared, the more I could see them being liberated from their pain. We then embraced them and spoke the Word of God to them, witnessing the great deliverance that came as the Spirit of God revealed the names of the specific roots that needed to be removed.

There was immediate freedom! The whole environment of the room changed as did the countenance of the people who released their stories and were relieved of their burdens, finding peace. They could finally smile again, after years of holding in their trauma. It was the most incredible encounter of inner healing that I have ever witnessed. Yes, Jesus Christ, the Hope of Glory is always there ready to heal and liberate!

A confirming Scripture to recall throughout your healing and throughout your life.

"The Spirit of the Lord God is upon Me,
Because the Lord has anointed Me to preach good tidings to
the poor;
He has sent Me to heal the brokenhearted.
To proclaim liberty to the captives,
And the opening of the prison to those who are bound;
To proclaim the acceptable year of the Lord,
And the day of vengeance of our God;
To comfort all who mourn, To console those who mourn in
Zion,
To give them beauty for ashes, The oil of joy for mourning,
The garment of praise for the spirit of heaviness;
That they may be called trees of righteousness,

The planting of the Lord, that He may be glorified."
And they shall rebuild the old ruins,
They shall raise up the former desolations,
And they shall repair the ruined cities,
The desolations of many generations.
Strangers shall stand and feed your flocks,
And the sons of the foreigner Shall be your plowmen and
your vinedressers.
But you shall be named the priests of the Lord,
They shall call you the servants of our God.
You shall eat the riches of the Gentiles, and in their glory
you shall boast.
Instead of your shame you shall have double honor,
And instead of confusion they shall rejoice in their portion.
Therefore, in their land they shall possess double;
Everlasting joy shall be theirs."
Isaiah 61:1-7 NKJV

These words speak of Jesus Christ Himself and His mission and purpose for coming to earth to redeem man. And in His Name, **I declare now to you that you are freed from your prison and that your brokenness is now being mended by the awesome hand of God! You shall now rise up out of your place of devastation, weeping and torment, restored in every area of your life!**

God is sending you help right now! For all the pain, guilt and shame you have experienced prior to this moment, you will receive double blessing! For your melancholy, confusion, and sadness you will rejoice and be happy once again!

Everlasting joy is now yours! Receive it in Jesus Name!

Chapter 3

Turning the Tides of Mourning

Whether we realize it or not we have been *mourning* and yes, grieving on the inside since the infliction of the abuse against us! We have been mourning the loss of our true selves, the self we would have been had we not suffered abuse.

When the enemy sees that our healing process has begun, he will throw lies and deceptive thoughts at us attempting to dr,ag us back under because he wants our suffering to leave us in a desolate place, feeling wasted and heavy of heart. But we are not destined to stay there!

To show us the way forward, the Lord gave me further insight into the complexity of wounded spirits. Our God sees us, each of us with a deep and abiding Love and clarity; and He is always present to guide us as we rebuild what was ruined. (Please re-read the Scripture at the end of chapter two.)

We are all born with a God-given purpose!

There is an event in Jesus' life told about in the Gospel of John (chapter 9), about a man who had been born blind. We know nothing about the man other than the opinions of the disciples who believed (as tradition taught them) that his blindness was caused by a sin he committed or that his parents committed. We know nothing about the man's attitude, either. However, placing ourselves in that situation, we can imagine that he felt alone, desolate and desperate, with a very heavy heart.

Like us, he most likely suffered physical, mental and emotional abuse. And like us, he probably believed that his life could never be different, so he wore the *masks* that were acceptable in his culture and he survived—part of the *unseen* people of the city. Satan must have been quite pleased.

Then Jesus brought His Light into that man's life saying, *"Neither this man nor his parents sinned, but this happened so that the works of God might be displayed in him."* The man's eyes were healed, and he experienced a total turnaround in his life. His neighbors took notice and celebrated with him! He was called before church leaders, who were spiritually blind and couldn't believe the miracle, so they threw him out. But Jesus came to him again, and strengthened him, setting him firmly on his path of Faith and God-given purpose.

"You have turned my mourning into joyful dancing.
You have taken away my clothes of mourning
and clothed me with joy,..."
Psalm 30: 11 (NLT)

Throughout thousands of years of human existence, there is much the Lord has helped us understand about the elements of grief and mourning; concepts that can be useful to those of us walking with Him through the process of healing.

In the 1960s, Elizabeth Kubler-Ross presented these concepts with fresh clarity. The first is shock/denial which we are all very familiar with, many of us screaming to ourselves, "This cannot be happening to me." We try to delete the incident and may be able to push it far away from conscious memory for a time. Should the incident happen again, the denial process repeats, sometimes causing what psychologists call "extremely fractured memories," triggering terrible nightmares and possibly mental illness. Satan works hard to send abuse victims down that road.

The second is anger. This strong human emotion throws Why and Who questions at us. "Why did this abuse happen to me?" "Who is to blame?" The term *slippery slope* applies here because once we allow the flames of anger to catch hold of us, the blame-game begins, and there is an almost infinite number of people who can be named as responsible for what we've suffered. Most of us start out believing we (ourselves) caused the abuse. Then Satan sends *hate* to sneak into view and our anger burns toward most everyone or everything including members of our family, or friends, or teachers as we begin to believe they could have stopped it. Again, the enemy of our souls loves to fan the flames anger and hate to keep those thoughts clogging our minds.

The third element within the grief/mourning process is bargaining. Oh, how we want to do anything to avoid dealing with our broken hearts—our broken spirits. "All that stuff in the past doesn't really bother me anymore." "Just let me get through today, and tomorrow I'll make an appointment with that counselor." But tomorrow doesn't come causing denial to set in deeper and the burning embers of anger to grow hotter.

The fourth component of mourning/grief is depression. There is no doubt that this is one of Satan's "big guns." Severe feelings of dejection and desolation can cause any of us to feel physically, mentally and spiritually ill. All we want to do (can do) is curl ourselves up in a relatively safe place and hide. Our hearts (spirits) are robbed of the health, peace and joy that God has given us—the life-giving elements that are our rightful inheritance now and forever, with Him. As we come to recognize this depression strategy of the enemy, we can finally see that we're participants in a *war* whether we've been aware of it or not. The best thing to remember is that Jesus has already

WON! And, through Him, we have won, too! What Jesus spoke to His disciples, He is saying to us, today: *"I have told you these things* [prepared you], *so that in Me you may have peace. In this world you will have trouble. But take heart! I have overcome the world."*

The last piece is a combination of testing and acceptance. Silent, long-time survivors of abuse might recognize this as a place of restless peace where they believe they can continue to *live* even if they are a shadow of the person they once were—or could be. Here we constantly *test the waters* of relationships and accept a passive lifestyle that won't stir up old memories. Many psychologist believe this is an excellent resolution that offers people relative happiness. Satan will also settle for this because the *uninvolved lifestyle* also keeps us numb to the Love and Life available to us from God. The enemy never wants us to experience the full *passion* of our God-given lives. Yet, hearing God's Word and His Promises to comfort us (with real comfort) and give us joy (real shout-to-the-rooftops joy) in place of our sadness, will break the back of passive acceptance.

These few lines from Scripture, given in the previous chapter, are balm to weary souls:

> He has sent Me to heal the brokenhearted.
> To proclaim liberty to the captives,
> And the opening of the prison to those who are bound;
> To comfort all who mourn,....
> To give them beauty for ashes, The oil of joy for mourning,
> The garment of praise for the spirit of heaviness;
> And instead of confusion they shall rejoice in their portion.
> Therefore, in their land they shall possess double;
> Everlasting joy shall be theirs."

These are the Promises God gives to us through His exquisite, unconditional Love for each individual (more about His Love in a later chapter). When a person comes to understand that Christ came to this earth to call us out of our prisons, we are assured that our broken hearts will be healed and restored! This is the Love of God made manifest through His Only Son, Jesus Christ.

God's Love mends all wounds! Of this I am a witness many times over! Although we may struggle with some of the recovery (processing) elements discussed in this chapter—maybe even experiencing them more than once—God's Love NEVER FAILS. He will bring us Victory!

~ ~ ~

While watching television one afternoon, I saw the story of an incredible musician, singer and songwriter named Billy Preston (1946-2006). I never knew his life story even though I was well aware of his music. Billy learned to play the organ at 9 years of age and became a prodigy within the church. He was an exceptional musician and singer and went on to find remarkable success in the R&B industry. He performed with Ray Charles, Mick Jagger, the Beatles and Eric Clapton. He also had several popular hits. Yet, Billy also had a painful secret.

As a young boy he was sexually abused. When family and friends finally learned about this, they concluded that since he had no outlet to share his pain, he was dying on the inside for all those many years. While his singing and playing were receiving accolades around the world, the little boy on the inside was tormented and crying, never finding a way to reach out for healing. Billy was perishing from *Internal Bleeding*.

The lifestyle of any 1960s musician was a hard one and even though Billy carried the seed of Faith in Christ, he fell prey to the deceptions of the enemy through the influence of peer pressure, drinking alcohol and using cocaine to try and soothe his pain. That abuse of drugs and alcohol eventually took his life. It breaks my heart to think how his earthly life would have changed had he been able to come to Jesus for complete healing.

Although Billy's story is one of hundreds that I know, personally, learning of his experiences has heightened my desire to pour into these pages all that God wants me to share, so that all victims of abuse can be restored to emotional, mental and spiritual health.

It also made me realize how important it is to reach out to boys and men who have suffered such incidents. Most often, the societal focus for compassion and assistance is on female abuse victims. There are however, many male victims of abuse that goes un-reported and remains hidden in secrecy.

Men who suffer verbal abuse or rejection by their fathers have a hard time coping and progressing in their mental, emotional and spiritual growth. Fathers have a tremendous responsibility to teach their sons what true manhood means, as they grow from infancy into mature men. How many Billy's are out there who are still too ashamed to share their stories with someone who could listen to and pray for them? How many continue to mourn the loss of who they might have been had they not been abused. So many people—grieving over their lost relationships, lost careers, lost dreams—are literally losing their lives because of one (or more) abuse incident(s). Don't allow yourself to continue being a statistic!

~ ~ ~

Before closing out this chapter on *Turning the Tides of Mourning*, I must make it clear that we are not fighting against the human perpetrators of our abuse, although there are certainly times when it is necessary to do so. The Holy Spirit inspired the Apostle Paul to tell us that...

"... we do not wrestle against flesh and blood, but against principalities,
against powers, against the rulers of the darkness of this age,
against spiritual hosts of wickedness in the heavenly places."
Ephesians 6:12 (NKJV)

The enemy (Satan) created the *spirit of abuse* to have no mercy! From those in the pulpit to the laity in church; from those in schools, charity work, business or politics; there are wounded women, men and children who have been brutally attacked. Too many are carrying fractured skeletons in their closets of untold stories that they desperately wish they could share. They wear their masques from the moment they wake up in the morning until they go to sleep at night. Burdened with Satan's lies, they cannot make spiritual progress, or find true peace because their past, keeps them in bondage—*internal bleeding* weakening every effort. Healthy and normal growth has been stunted. Their pure spirit has been contaminated and a lifestyle of self-hatred twists and contorts normal social and sexual behavior into promiscuity.

We must not just stem this tide, we must turn it back on itself, seeking God's Power to carefully watch over us, our children and loved ones, and uncover abuse of all kinds wherever it is found. So, I'm asking you to RISE UP! Remove the blinders Satan has placed around your spiritual heart. Speak out (1st to God and yourself) about what has happened to you and fight back.

If you feel trapped in an abusive relationship, do not listen to the enemy's deceptive lies that "no one cares," or that "everyone will know you're the cause." You can escape that torment in the Name of Jesus Christ! Today is your opportunity to tell yourself the Truth about Who really loves you, who you are in His family and who you're meant to be. Today is your day to Turn the Tide of your Mourning into *dancing*!

Jesus Christ, The Living Son of God, can and will make you whole and free again. His Power is more than able to transform and restore you to a place of newness, health and prosperity. And with that transformation He will give you His Perfect Peace! He is the Prince of Peace! It will be as if the trauma in your life never occurred. Of that, I personally testify! **If you** can believe and receive Him, His Love will make you complete and erase the pain.

I declare that as you read this book God will set you free from your mental, emotional and physical torment! This is my daily prayer for you! Today, you are released from your silence!

If you want to cry out to God right now, do just that. The God of heaven and earth sent His Son Jesus Christ to ensure that you could be free, because He bore your pain and grief. He is listening and will embrace and heal you by the Power of His Love!

If you have painful memories of child abuse, or any form of abuse that you are still holding onto, it is time to let go and receive God's free gift of healing and liberation. This moment is your opportunity to say out loud. "God, I was abused. I will no longer be a victim of that abuse!"

I believe if you have read this far you are feeling some relief already. Memories are flooding your mind, and maybe some tears are flowing. But everything is about to change for the better! Even now you can make this declaration! HEALED AM I!!

Pray this prayer: Father in the name of Jesus Christ, I come to you broken, wounded, and hurting deeply as a result of the abuse committed against me. I give all of it to You now and ask that You heal my heart, heal my mind and restore my soul! Amen.

A confirming Scripture to recall throughout your healing process ~ throughout your life.

For He was wounded for our transgressions, bruised for our iniquities,
the chastisement of our peace was upon Him and
by His stripes, we are healed."
Isaiah 53:5

Christ's suffering, His death on the Cross and His Resurrection made the Way for us to be healed in every area of our lives. I give Glory to God for His Provision, Grace and Mercy in my

life and in the lives of all who reach out to Him for His Redeeming Love.

Chapter 4

Confronting the Enemy-Part One

God's Way to Fight, Stand Our Ground, and Win!
"Therefore, take up the whole armor of God,
that you may be able to withstand in the evil day,
and having done all, to stand."
Ephesians 6:13

For anyone who has been abused, confrontation is never an easy thing to consider, let alone actually do. But for your safety, I must say this first. **IF you are in a situation where you feel you (or someone else in the house) is in immediate danger, please call 911, or go to a sanctuary location—a church, hospital or fire station.** I am praying for you, and never want you to be harmed again.

~ ~ ~

In my experience, there seems to be something about the very thought of actually confronting our abuser(s) that may set in motion a more severe attack. However, I am here to tell you today that doing so is a major step toward total freedom physically, mentally and spiritually and there are steps you can take to prepare.

The first and most crucial step is to strengthen and equip ourselves spiritually. By this I mean, speaking the truth of what happened to you, to yourself and to God (as suggested earlier) and releasing everything into His Hands. The Lord then begins to teach us how to discover the *armor* He's prepared for us, and how to utilize each *piece* to the fullest.

As we grow to understand that God wants us to be completely free from any and all forms of bondage, especially the bondage of abuse and that the Greater One (God) dwells within us, we can prevail against Satan and walk in the peace and healing that is rightfully ours. The "weapons that were formed against us" can no longer prosper!

> *"But no weapon that is formed against you shall prosper,*
> *and every tongue that shall rise against you in judgment*
> *you shall show to be in the wrong.*
> *This* peace, righteousness, security, triumph over opposition
> *is the heritage of the servants of the Lord*
> those in whom the ideal Servant of the Lord is reproduced;
> *this is the righteousness or the vindication which they obtain*
> *from Me*
> this is that which I impart to them as their justification,
> *says the Lord."*
> Isaiah 54:17 (AMPC)

The Lord also shows us how the enemy of our souls was deceiving and manipulating the perpetrator of the abuse against us. With our cooperation, He will lead us to forgive the person(s) who attacked us, which in turn brings us more peace and a closer relationship with God. But make no mistake, our God *hates* what has been done to us.

> *A jealous and avenging God is the Lord;*
> *The Lord is avenging and wrathful....*
> *The Lord is slow to anger and great in power,*

And the Lord will by no means leave the guilty unpunished.

Nahum 1-3 (NASB)

Yes, God is extremely angry at the evil, injustice, and damage that has come against you. And we can, indeed, be confident that He will keep us safe.

"Because of the devastation of the afflicted,
because of the groaning of the needy,
Now I will arise," says the Lord;
"I will set him in the safety for which he longs."

Psalm 12:5 (NASB)

We can also be assured that we will not be confronting the human abuser, or the enemy of our souls, alone. We have Jesus Christ, the Son of God, His shed Blood and the Word of God the Father, plus all the hosts of heaven to defend us! It is vital that you understand this at this crossroads of Faith and that you accept Jesus Christ as your personal Savior, if you have not already done so. **Bringing the King of kings and the Lord of lords into your camp is key to your freedom on earth and into eternity.**

If you are willing right now to accept Jesus Christ into your heart, *"He is faithful and just to forgive"* (1 John 1:9). Not only will personal sins be erased, but He will now have your permission to begin erasing all evidence of the abuse you experienced! His Love for us is like no love on this earth! Receive Christ into your heart now, by praying this simple prayer:

Dear Father God, I need You. My life and my heart are terribly broken. Today, I've finally come to realize that You have better plans for me, better ways of living than I can even imagine right now. I want to live my life with Your Son, Jesus, in it. I know that His sacrifice, death on the cross, and resurrection have made the Way for me to become a new creation, in Him. I choose now to accept Your mercy through Jesus, Your Son, as the Way, the Truth and the Life. I place myself, my life and my future into Your Hands. Please be my Teacher and Guide forever. Amen.

Praise God! You are now firmly, completely, absolutely part of God's Family, supported by His Grace, Mercy, Love and Almighty Power – and ready to prepare to confront the human perpetrator of your abuse.

However, before we move too quickly in that direction, there is more good news to share. Stepping into relationship with God, and His Son, Jesus, also introduces the Holy Spirit into our lives and His counsel is inspiring and powerful!

Jesus prepared His disciples—and us—for the time when He would not be physically upon this earth by announcing the arrival of the Holy Spirit. He said: *I will ask the Father, and He will give you another Helper, that He may be with you forever; that is the Spirit of Truth, Whom the world cannot receive, because it does not see Him or know Him, but you know Him because He abides with you and will be in you....But the Helper, the Holy Spirit, whom the Father will send in My name, He will teach you all things, and bring to your remembrance all that I said to you.* (John 14: 16-17, 26)

This is so exciting! Even though the Holy Spirit always existed with the Father and Son, He now becomes even more active in the lives of believers; being our Helper, Comforter, Counselor, Teacher and Revealer of Truth. It is through Him we learn about "the armor of God" and how to "put it on" for our protection, in preparation to meet the challenges of this world and in preparation to confront any abuser(s) whether human or spirit.

The Apostle Paul knew the value of such help after he accepted Jesus into his life and in his letter to the Ephesians (6:10-11, 14-17) he encourages us today with these words:

Finally, my brethren, be strong in the Lord and in the power of His might. Put on the whole armor of God, that you may be able to stand against the wiles of the devil....

*Stand therefore, having **girded your waist with truth**, having **put on the breastplate of righteousness**, and having **shod your feet with the preparation of the gospel of peace**; above all, **taking the shield of faith** with which you will be able to quench all the fiery darts of the wicked one. And **take the helmet of salvation**, and the **sword of the Spirit, which is the Word of God**;...*

Paul's descriptive phrasing here gives us the image of the pieces of a Roman soldier's protective armor, relating each piece to the spiritual elements we need to have, hold on to, and strengthen throughout our lifetime, for our own protection and the protection of others.

- **Having girded your waist with truth**. The visual image presented to us here is the piece of armor that not only carries the scabbard (which holds the sword), but also cinches the breastplate in place. Without it a soldier would go into battle, defenseless. This compares to the preparation we need, spiritually; to "gird" ourselves with the God-inspired Truths found in the Bible (both Old and New Testaments). These facts join together to become our spiritual "belt" (piece of equipment or tool) that will strengthen us in all parts of our life, especially as the Holy Spirit shows us the Truth of situations, protecting us from the lies and deceptions of Satan.
- **Having put on the breastplate of righteousness**. I know a lot of people who get distracted by the word

"righteousness." Throughout more recent generations, Satan has tainted the concept of that word to mean one group of people who believe they are "better than" or "more favored by God" than other human beings. That wrong perception has contaminated many relationships and set an obstacle in the way to the revelation of who we really are. The accurate (and simple) definition of *righteousness* is *doing what is right in God's eyes*. This can be a challenge for most of us. However, when we align ourselves with Him and His Ways,we recognize that the commands He gives us are based on His total and unconditional Love for us. Obeying them is like wearing the soldier's "breastplate" that protects the central vital body organs and most specifically our spiritual lives from fatal attacks.

· **Having shod your feet with the preparation of the Gospel of Peace**. If you're like me, when my feet hurt, my whole body hurts. My attitude, and motivation to move forward also suffers. This statement (this command) encourages us to *be prepared* for the journey we'll be walking out in life; to allow the Gospel message—everything Jesus said and did, and everything the Holy Spirit inspired the Apostles to write about—to prepare us. So that, in the very midst of tragedy and consequences of worldly sins, we can experience God's Peace. His Gospel (His Story) gives us purpose and focus, showing us the real meaning of life on this planet and beyond—one step at a time.

· **Taking the shield of faith with which you will be able to quench all the fiery darts of the wicked one**. This statement has always energized me because I can vividly imagine a huge *shield* that is held in front of me, made of God's impenetrable Power, protecting me from head to toe. This piece of spiritual armor is also a piece of weaponry that not only deflects attacks but sends the enemy's "fiery darts" ricocheting back in their direction. However, we must understand, that our Faith (our belief in God) is a choice we must make every day, to take it up (pick up our Faith) and place it in front of us where it can function as God intends in every part of our lives.

· **Take the helmet of salvation**. All the illustrations I've seen of the helmets of Roman soldiers show variations of metal *surrounding* as much of the head as possible; top, back, sides, even down and across the cheekbone and jaw areas and most are tightly secured with a leather strap. This image is what the Holy Spirit brings to us, demonstrating that our *salvation* (our redemption that was bought for us by the stripes, death and resurrection of Jesus, the Son of God) is the supernatural protection we possess; and which safeguards our minds from every assault of the enemy! The confidence and knowledge we have in our salvation, our restored place/position with God—allows us to walk in the Power of the Holy Spirit as we live the lives we've always been meant to have; in clarity of mind and discernment of persons, places and things that the enemy attempts to send against us.

· **Take the Sword of the Spirit, which is the Word of God**. The sword of a Roman soldier was his first and basic offensive weapon. It is said in the history books that it was their swords "that conquered the world," having two sharpened edges and a tapered point that could pierce even the strongest metal armor of their enemies. So it is with the WORD of God. We need no other weapons because (1) God's Word reveals all

Truth, the good, bad and ugly. His Word *lives* as Jesus, Himself, is alive; powerful and "sharper than any two-edged sword" showing us Truth from lies and the intent of the hearts of men. The Word of God cuts to the core, dividing the enemy's forces and uncovering their plots. This is a close combat weapon that can be relied on to get us through any assault. There is no demonic force that can withstand it!

With these brief descriptions, I pray that you'll be inspired by the Holy Spirit to accept the Armor He's given us. With each and every thought that we turn toward God, toward His Love for us and His Compassionate Provisions. We turn our back on Satan and the destruction he sends against us. My personal spiritual warfare abilities strengthen daily as I "put on" these weapons, and I know they will fortify you, too.

~ ~ ~

As you and the Holy Spirit work together, setting your armor in place and building your spiritual strength, I must mention another spiritual element that will bless you: FORGIVENESS.

It is extremely important to understand that *unforgiveness* prevents us from being free! When we don't forgive the person(s) who have hurt and abused us, we remain imprisoned and our way forward is hindered. We block the Grace and Power of God to fully restore us.

"But if you do not forgive others their trespasses
their reckless and willful sins, leaving them, letting them go, and giving up resentment,
neither will your Father forgive you your trespasses."
Matthew 6:15 (AMPC)

Forgiving an abuser or anyone for that matter is truly a Divine act. As a believer in Jesus Christ, we forgive by and through the power of the Holy Spirit within us. In our own humanity we are incapable of true forgiveness. Forgiveness of those who have wronged us truly sets us free.

We can understand God's forgiveness because we have been forgiven much and now stand righteous before Him because of Christ's sacrifice. If you have never experienced God's forgiveness, it will be impossible for you to forgive anyone.

The real truth is that without God's Love working in us we cannot release true forgiveness. Our own forgiveness is conditional and incomplete, because we are limited by our humanity in efforts to wipe the slate clean. This fact is the foundation for most roots of bitterness in our lives. Because of Christ's sacrifice for us on the Cross and His resurrection, all our sins are forgiven. Even as we walk toward Him and prepare ourselves to ask, He has already forgiven us! That is an amazing love bestowed upon us by God the Father!

For if you forgive people their trespasses
their reckless and willful sins, leaving them, letting them
go, and giving up resentment,
your heavenly Father will also forgive you.
Matthew 6:14 (AMPC)

It is important to realize that the person used by the enemy to harm us was not the enemy. Abuse and perversion are demonic spirits that control a person who is not walking with the Spirit of God. This is not to say that the person is totally relieved from the responsibility of their actions, but they were used by the enemy and yielded themselves to his suggestions and the lusts of their flesh. They carried out unnatural acts, physically, verbally and emotionally abusing others.

So, forgiving our abusers can be made easier when we separate the sin from the sinner—when we realize that the abuser also needs deliverance for their soul, and may also have been a victim in their past. This does not justify their evil, abusive behavior but can help us understand the nature of their state of mind and their need for the Grace of God.

Forgiveness takes place in your heart and spirit. It releases you to move forward with your life and your process of restoration. However, the Divine ability to forgive the abuser comes from God and is His gift to us—which we must choose to accept. This is an important key to complete wholeness and for-ever-freedom from the *internal bleeding* and *mourning* we've been experiencing.

Forgiveness closes the door to the offense(s) preventing them from ever returning. It also slams the door in Satan's face—the enemy of our souls—so that he can no longer torment us. Below is a prayer that I've shared with many victims.

Prayer of Forgiveness and Release

Father, in Jesus' Holy Name, I come to You, today, saying out loud that I was abused by_____. His/her assault against me wounded me so deeply and now I want to be healed and set free from the torment of my soul. Father, because You love me and gave your Son for me as sacrifice, I know that by the stripes of Jesus I am healed. I receive Your healing in my heart, in my soul, and in my emotions. Cleanse me now completely of every root of abuse, every wound of bitterness, and give me the mind of Christ. Restore my soul!

I forgive _____, so that his/her presence in my life or memory of the abuse can no longer have any power over me! I declare that I am healed and made whole by the Power of the Holy Spirit. In Jesus Name! Amen!

Chapter 5

Confronting the Enemy-Part Two

God's Way to Prepare Us to Confront Our Human Abusers,
In tandem with spiritually preparing ourselves, we may also need to formulate a plan to confront the actual person(s) who abused us. If the incidents have been reported to the police, there may already be prosecutors talking with you about your testimony in a court of law. If family members have discovered what has been happening, they may have made the choice to call authorities, kick the abuser out of the house, or even "run away" from the situation, not wanting any other confrontation. There is also the possibility that the perpetrator may be deceased while the painful memories are alive and well in your mind and soul. Many other circumstantial possibilities exist; however, it is my belief (and experience) that confronting the person who harmed us is a course of action that ultimately benefits everyone.

If we allow *fear* to keep us locked up and immobilized (silenced) it becomes a cancer that contaminates and poisons our soul deep within us. Yet, discovering who we are—God's beloved child—we come to the realization that freedom from

fear and abuse is our right! Our Father/God wants us to move
forward into a better life made whole as we fulfill the pur-
pose(s) for which we were born.

For the remainder of this chapter I will offer you several
pieces of strategy that I know will help you overcome fear and
confront your abuser. You may want to grab a pen and some
paper. Writing down your responses to the questions will help
you keep focused as memories begin to surface. You may want
to read through the questions first before starting to write. Remember, this book and each chapter in it has been prepared to
help you and *release you* from the bondage of abuse. There is
no time limit to the process. Only you can decide when to begin this part of the process and God is with you in the midst of
every moment!

Who was/is the abuser(s)? I knew my abusers and wrote
their names here. I also added who they are/were to me, the
position/role they held in my life (family member, friend).

How and when did the abuse begin? Writing about the first
time my abuser approached me was, indeed, painful. However,
because I'd already been talking with God about it, I felt His
cocoon of Love and His assurance that He would give me the
strength to get through this.

Where did it happen? In more than one location? I was able
to recall the exact places. When I became a counselor, I realized that *isolation* was a key factor. The abuser always found a
location that hid his actions. Knowing this fact has helped me
warn potential victims and keep them safe.

Was the abuse over a period of time? When I answered "Yes"
to this question, I also wrote a long paragraph about my ages at
the times of the assaults. The early childhood abuse happened
between the ages of 6 and 8, while another attack happened in
my college years. I've often wondered if I had found a way to
tell someone about the earlier events, could I have been better

prepared to avoid the last one?

Many people only have flashes of remembrance and that is alright. The following questions will continue to help you recover the memories that are necessary to reveal so that you can move forward.

Are your memories vivid or vague flashbacks?My memories were both vague and extremely vivid. Some elements of the attacks against me were so intense that I could smell the shampoo he'd used. Others were hazy images that I found hard to identify. Can you recall the emotions you felt? Write down all of the emotions you experienced at the time, and throughout the days/months/years afterward.

This is particularly important for those of us who kept silent about the abuse for many years. Emotions are meant to be a blessing in our lives. Yet, after being attacked we naturally respond by either shutting down our emotions or letting them get out of control.

For me, personally, I did my best to hold my emotions in check. I hated my abuser and yet loved him at the same time. This caused me quite a bit of stress, guilt, fear, shame, anger, and anxiety, and I built relationship barriers that I thought would protect me.

Have you ever considered what pain that person (those people) might have experienced that caused them to become abusive? If asked this question as a child, the answer would have been a resounding "No." However, I'm not certain the "no" was accurate. I've come to understand that there is an internal bucket of compassion within the majority of human beings that (more often than not) causes us to consider what "the other guy feels."

I now believe that God's ways of healing the abuse victims also extends to healing the abusers. I will briefly address this in a later chapter. Did you ever confront them or try and tell someone about what happened to you? My response to this question is "YES!" Somewhere around the age of seven or eight, I approached another relative and actually spoke the word "abuse" to her. I was immediately "shushed" and told that she didn't believe I knew what I was saying—and to never repeat it again.

However, if I could go back in time, I would find someone else to tell; someone I knew would listen to me and believe me. I had already built walls of silence around myself, and that person who *shushed* me built them even higher, locking me in an invisible prison that damaged me, and many other relationships, even more.

Have you been able to forgive the abuser? Today, I can honestly answer "Yes" to this question. Yet, I am well aware that this forgiveness is a reality only because of my daily walk with the Lord. The enemy of our eternal lives still (occasionally) attempts to draw me back into the emotion of hatred with an ugly memory.

However, if I were responding to this question in the early stages of my recovery and restoration, the answer would be "No." I could acknowledge that forgiving that person(s) was necessary. I could believe that I would eventually get there. But I wasn't even close to forgiving them at that time.

What result are you seeking? Before confronting the abuser, consider your expectations. As I've walked with many people through the *confrontation* possibilities, I continue to learn the importance of this piece of planning, even though every eventuality cannot be anticipated. For me, after 30 years of silence, I really had no idea what to expect from the abuser or my family. So, I gave my human expectations to God and relied on His Grace to calm the storm.

These are a few things to think about and prepare for: What if the abuser apologizes? Asks for forgiveness? Repents out-loud to you and God? Will you expect them to turn themselves into police and answer for their crime(s) against you?

What if they don't show any indications of remorse at all? Will you tell them that you are going to the authorities (or have gone to authorities) and that police are waiting to arrest them? What if they react with a violent outburst? Deny everything? Throw accusations back at you? Threaten to sue you for liable? Have you brought someone with you who can physically protect you? What if the confrontation does not bring you the immediate closure you expected? Will you seek (continue) counseling to help you reach that point and move past it? Do you want an answer to "Why" they abused you? Most perpetrators don't know how to respond to that "Why" question because they've either been denying the fact that they did it, or they've been deceived into believing that they had no power to stop it. If they can't (or won't) give you an answer, how will that effect your resolve to move out of the past?

When you're ready—and only when you are mentally, emotionally, physically and spiritually ready—to confront your abuser, here are a few additional ways to prepare.

Plan the time of day and the place. This moment of coming face-to-face with that person is happening for your benefit. It is part of your recovery process—not theirs—and your physical and emotional well-being is important. Select a time of day when you normally feel at your peek. Select a place that is comfortable, peaceful, with good lighting and temperature. These boundaries will create a safe environment for you.

Do everything you can to prepare yourself to *feel* the emotions of abuse, again. Even now as you ponder these questions many feelings, thoughts, memories, places and faces have probably come to your mind and spirit. Forgotten experiences may have surfaced. But keep in mind that your goal is to say what you want to say to that person and ask your questions. Working with your counselor, a pastor, or friend to "role play" this day is an excellent preparation tool. You can even write down your specific questions or comments and take them with you. Remember, you are not "confronting" a friend, and there is no need to impress them by pretending you are okay.

Call them OUT! Tell them that what they did to you was a sin against you, against God, and a criminal offense that requires justice. Circumstances vary widely at this point depending on the length of time that has passed between the time of abuse and the present. However, *justice* is definitely one of the main goals of most victims. While the statute of limitations for child abuse in the U.S. varies by state, Federal law is for as long as the victim is alive or for 10 years after the event, whichever is longer (U.S. Code 18, Section 3283). I've known people who have selected a friend to accompany them at the time of the confrontation who also happened to be a police officer, and they gave the abuser the opportunity to turn themselves in.

If the situation presents itself—and you are inclined to do so—be prepared to pray with that person. This not only will increase your Peace, it makes Satan really mad! Giving an abuser an opportunity to turn their lives over to God is a big win in the Kingdom of Heaven. Tell them that there is *a spirit of abuse* that they must be freed from; a stronghold that is joined by several other spirits (guilt, torment, sadness, anger, depression and shame). Then invite them to say this basic prayer for their salvation: *Father God, I present myself before You seeking Your forgiveness. Thank You for sending your Son, Jesus, to die on the Cross for me, taking my place of punishment for my sin of abuse against this woman (man) and against You, Lord, and for all the other sins I've committed. From this moment, and for the rest of my life, I ask Jesus to come into my life and free me; to make me a new creation in Him. I believe in you, Jesus, and Your Power and Authority to cleanse me and de-*

clare me forgiven. I am set free and cleansed by the blood of Je-
sus! Amen!

Praying those words with/for your abuser will be a deeply emotional experience—for both of you. However, if you were unable to do so, another alternative is to have the prayer written out and give it to them when you leave. God's Grace is alive and active no matter when the moment comes, and your willingness to simply place the prayer in their hand will lift much of the heaviness from your shoulders.

Here is one last thought to conclude this chapter. The preparations suggested here deal directly with confronting a reachable or "living" abuser. However, there are ways to confront the abuser who is deceased, in prison, completely unknown to you, or not safe to be near. One of the best ways is to write a letter, possibly several letters to that person expressing what you need to say and the questions you need to ask. These letters never have to be sent, but if they are, you must prepare yourself for the consequences just as you did to confront them in person. If this is your situation, I pray that you're working with an excellent counselor who can assist you with this.

NOW, please allow me to pray for you.

May the Peace of God cover you like a toasty, warm blanket wherever you are and give you strength that you never thought was possible! May His Presence, here with you this very moment, give you the Grace to maneuver through these times. May the Glory Light of Jesus Christ shine in your heart and mind and destroy any darkness surrounding you. You are no longer a victim, but a brand new you! Together, we give God the Glory. In Jesus' Name. Amen.

> *"For God has not given us a spirit of fear, but of power,*
> *love and a sound mind."*
> 2 Timothy 1:7 (NKJV)

Chapter 6

There Is Wisdom In Counsel

Yet I am always with You;
You hold me by my right hand.
You guide me with Your counsel,
Psalm 73:23-24 (NIV)

Counseling and psychology have not always been looked upon with favor. Many people have developed their opinions from newspaper headlines that expose a counselor who has abused their position and harmed their patients. Yet in my experience, the counselors I've known have given their entire lives to helping people discover relief and restoration from their problems. I also know that the majority of Christian counselors continually place their efforts in God's Hands—seeking His Counsel with and for their clients. Scripture gives us multiple *words of wisdom* advising us to *seek counsel*, and I can do no less.

I managed to hide my pain for many years; to lock myself in a secret prison of silence. To my knowledge, no one had any inkling that I was abused. I kept silent until my early thirties when (as I shared in chapter one) I cried out to God and His

Healing Grace freed me. At that point I was not led to connect with a professional psychologist or counselor. However, the Lord did lead me into a counseling/praying relationship with one of His highly trained Prophetesses who He'd prepared (in advance) to meet me and my needs. Later, the Lord, also introduced me to a Pastor in another country who has become a counselor and prayer partner, who I can confide in when facing the tough times of daily life.

With transparency, I share these things with you so that you will know that our Faithful and Loving Father/God knows each of us so well (better than we know ourselves); and offers each of us His healing when we are willing to accept it. Like physical healings from God, some people receive instant miracles, and some receive miracles that take place over time, through a process. In both instances, the Holy Spirit remains with us continuing to provide us with His counsel, plus the counsel of people He deems to place in our paths for a specific season.

So, I say to you today, it is never too late to cry out and reach out to God and His human counselors for further assistance in becoming completely free from your personal trauma. And I declare to you now that you are already receiving excellent *counsel* from God in your heart and mind and are more prepared than ever before to receive the restoration and peace you long for.

~ ~ ~

Being able to go and speak with a trusted individual who is capable of carefully listening to how you really feel inside is a blessing from God. These people do a great service by just *listening* to us. Many call this *counseling* a "sacred gift." Recently I came across this quote from the courageous Christian, Dietrich Bonhoeffer:

"Just as love to God begins with listening to His Word, so the beginning of love for the brethren is learning to listen to them."

Dietrich Bonhoeffer, *Life Together* (New York: Harper & Row, 1954), 97-8.

I believe that God has given some very special people this gift of *listening* (counseling) and it is a wise thing to seek out this ministry. This is especially true for those who have kept their abuse a secret—locked away and festering—for years. The *internal bleeding* and *mourning* must STOP! Speaking with a counselor may be the next big step toward "getting it all out of your system."

From my own experience of sharing my heart with several people the Holy Spirit directed me to—and the struggles of those I've counseled—I know that dreams, nightmares, fear, depression and flashbacks plague the victims of abuse. This is like sleeping with (cooperating with) the enemy as Satan continues to seek our destruction. We know that something is just not right. We try to get through our days peacefully, yet something is eating at us, gnawing at us from the inside. We've tried to stuff the memories so far down that they will never surface. Yet liberty has not come, and we continue to suffer.

Through counseling we learn that most of the distress we experience is a result of *the root* of pain and abuse that has grown up like a weed inside of our spirits. When we accept the misery, and attempt to ignore it, telling ourselves that "This is the way things will always be," we will continue to experience the painful symptoms. The focus now must be to uproot the root!

Of additional concern is that, because of the deep and tangled roots of past pain and abuse, we may also remain in unhealthy relationships and have no ability to walk away from them. The thought processes needed to take the logical steps of escape from that situation, even for our own safety or the protection of children, has been torn apart and crushed. So, once again, I repeat, *"God has not given us a spirit of fear, but of power, love and a sound mind."* And He has provided the "sacred gift" of counseling ministries to help us. If this is your situation today, please seek help. If there is immediate danger to yourself or other family members call 911. If the danger is not immediate, ask them to connect you with a local Crisis Center counselor, and allow the Holy Spirit to direct you to the right person in this moment.

~ ~ ~

When feeling the heaviness of guilt and shame that falls upon every survivor of abuse, we often believe that weight can never be removed or even lessened. However, I tell you today that those feelings are direct attacks from the spirits of oppression that Satan sets against us. Many times, even after working through anger and bitterness to reach the point of forgiving our abusers—and healing has begun—these two arrows continue to pierce us.

As mentioned earlier, my counseling process was in a cocooned place with the Holy Spirit. However, eventually He led me to talk with one very special friend, Prophetess Mary Johnson-Gordon, whose words of wisdom and prayers helped me break free from all demonic oppression and walk in God's freedom.

One of the Scriptures she directed me to is in the Book of Acts, chapter 3. It is about the day a lame man (who had been lame since birth) was carried and left at the main gate of his town—where they "put him" every day. In those days, it was generally believed that anyone with a handicap had been cursed by God (one of those deceiving lies the enemy perpetuates even today). Every physically or mentally challenged person grew up understanding what their neighbors thought of them and they were filled with guilt and shame (not God's plan for anyone).

When the Apostles, Peter and John, were about to enter the city, the lame man noticed someone was walking toward him and asked them for money (his normal way of making a living). Peter and John then looked directly at the man and Peter said, *"Look at us!"* This indicates that the man had looked away from them as soon as he anticipated them coming near. Here is how Scriptures describes the rest of what happened.

"So the man gave them his attention, expecting to get something from them.

Then Peter said, 'Silver or gold I do not have, but what I do have I give you.

In the name of Jesus Christ of Nazareth, walk.'

Taking him by the right hand, he helped him up, and instantly the man's feet and ankles became strong.

He jumped to his feet and began to walk.

Then he went with them into the temple courts, walking and jumping, and

praising God. When all the people saw him walking and praising God, they recognized

him as the same man who used to sit begging at the temple gate called Beautiful,

and they were filled with wonder and amazement at what had happened to him.

While the man held on to Peter and John, all the people were astonished

and came running to them in the place called Solomon's Colonnade.

Acts 3:5-11 (NIV)

Although this man had been lame from birth, and was deeply affected by shame and guilt, he made the decision to look up, receive his healing, get up, and rise out of his *lame place.* It is the same with our private prisons that have been created by our pain and layered with our insecurities and fears.

Right at this moment, you may feel trapped and weighted with guilt and shame. It is imperative for you to know that God has made a way of escape for you. **All you need to do is agree with Who God says He is, who He says you are (His beloved child), and What He tells us He can do.** Yes, it is time. Rise up inside and see your prison door open! God is the Liberator! Through and by the power of His Spirit you can be completely free.

In the Name of Jesus, I break the power of the spirits of guilt and shame over your mind, body, soul, and spirit! Be set free by the power of God! May the Blood of Jesus Christ now wash you and cleanse you from all demonic oppression. May peace, joy, and confidence now fill your spirit by the Power of the Holy Spirit. In the name of Jesus!

~ ~ ~

One more thing about the shame and guilt the enemy attempts to smother us with: God has given us His Eternal Promise that we will be given double the joy and double the beauty to replace it! I must repeat the following Scripture here, to remind us just how much God wants to heal us and has set His plans in motion to also restore us! The Prophet, Isaiah, reveals what God inspired him to write, saying:

He [God the Father] *has sent Me* [Jesus] *to heal the broken-*
hearted,
...To give them beauty for ashes,
The oil of joy for mourning,
The garment of praise for the spirit of heaviness;
That they may be called trees of righteousness,
The planting of the Lord, that He may be glorified....
Instead of your shame you shall have double honor,
And instead of confusion they shall rejoice in their portion.
Therefore, in their land they shall possess double;
Everlasting joy shall be theirs."
Isaiah 61:1, 3 & 7

When God does His restorative work in our souls it is Divine surgery! It is complete and irreversible! He doesn't bring us just to a place of healing but of wholeness. There is an undeniable sense of peace and quiet in our heart and spirit when we confess our pain to Him and open our hearts and emotions to Him. The Scripture above speaks of a great exchange; beauty for ashes, the oil of joy for mourning and the garment of praise of the spirit of heaviness! See yourself in your minds' eye being transformed by these words! See your painful past being exchanged for a glorious light. See yourself restored anew and whole.

God truly is the mender of broken hearts! When a ravaged, torn and broken heart is mended and restored to a healthy state, this is truly a miracle! He restores our self-image, which really is (and has been since our spirits came into existence) a reflection of His image – the Image of Christ! We rise from our ashes and walk right out of our tombs and what people see is the glory of God.

You may not realize it but all you have experienced is for someone else's victory. That may be difficult to understand at the moment you're reading this book, nonetheless, once restored to wholeness, you have a unique testimony of not just survival but of freedom and liberation that only you can tell. Your story will help to liberate others! If you are in Christ and are living for Him, your devastation and pain has been turned into the oil of healing that is going to flow out of you for the benefit of others. **God is not only giving you back your life, but He is giving you a richer, dynamic and more abundant life! This is why Christ came!**

This is the prayer I pray with others who are claiming God's Isaiah 61 Promises:

> Lord, I pray now according to Isaiah 61 that You would give me beauty for my ashes. Take all of the things that were meant to destroy me and remove

them from my life. Give me the oil of joy for the mourning that overshadowed my soul. Let me now be saturated in Your joy which is full and complete. I can breathe freely and smile again because of the peace You bring. Clothe me now in the garment of praise which I exchange for the garment of heaviness. I will lift my heart and my hands and be thankful to God for setting me free. In place of all the shame and anguish that I have carried for so long, I thank You as You give me a double portion of Your blessing, peace, joy and restoration. My past is over, and my best days are ahead of me. I shall live and not die. Amen.

I am so very thankful for God's counsel and the counsel of the uniquely prepared peopled He has placed in my life. May you, too, enjoy these blessings from our Father.

~ ~ ~

The following chapters offer more information about counseling and some of the statistics that continue to impress upon my heart how very much we all need to walk with the LORD, daily.

Chapter 7

Psychology Concepts and Statistics of Interest

Personally, I have found it helpful to look at abuse from the psychological perspective. This has given me a clearer picture of how the enemy infiltrates the soul where our emotions (love, hate, fear, joy, etc.), mind (intellect), and will (decision-making ability) reside.

First looking at human emotions, beginning in childhood, I came across this disturbing (but accurate) piece of information.

> "Emotional abuse is a pattern of behavior that attacks a child's emotional development and sense of self-worth. Emotional abuse includes excessive, aggressive or unreasonable demands that place expectations on a child beyond his or her capacity. Constant criticizing, belittling, insulting, rejecting and teasing are some of the forms these verbal attacks can take. Emotional abuse also includes failure to provide the psychological nurturing

necessary for a child's psychological growth and development—providing no love, support or guidance."

(National Committee for the Prevention of Child Abuse, 1987).

It is important to take special note of that last sentence. Neglect ("failure to provide") is most definitely a form of abuse. We are hearing more and more in the news about cases where children and the elderly are being ignored, locked in closets, and starved causing lasting damage to them physically and to their sense of well-being.

An opposite side of neglect is "bullying." In schools all across America and around the world children experience verbal and physical threats, feeling intimidated by the aggressive behavior of one, or several people. Recently we've come to recognize there are other, more subtle forms of bullying such as harassment that extends into social media which includes Facebook and online chat rooms. Authorities are now naming this type of bullying as a contributing factor in teen and young adult suicides.

Below are lists of symptoms that manifest in children and adults who have been emotionally abused. I have placed beside the indicators, the correlating spiritual attacks that come from the enemy to further inflict damage upon a person who manifests these symptoms. Our medical physicians, psychiatrists and psychologist/counselors can assist in identifying these behaviors and, if necessary, diagnosing brain abnormalities and/or mental illnesses.

Please take note that some of the indicators listed below may also apply to a growing population who have been born with brain anomalies and have been diagnosed with down syndrome, autism, are savants or have other brain-related differences. These special people (as well as every living person) needs Holy Spirit guidance so that Satan cannot choke out their unique Kingdom Purposes. Every living person has been given God's extraordinary gifts, talents, and spiritual insights "for such a time as this," and needs the support of discerning parents, family and friends to help navigate the storms of life.

Within every personal circumstance, God's Truth can reveal the *root* of any demonic activity that might be behind the behavior(s). When the root is allowed to grow, the fruit of our lives can be damaged or destroyed. Only when that root is exposed and *uprooted* can there be permanent change and liberation. The Word of God tells us that, "Who the Son sets free is free indeed," and He sets us free through many methods, through the work of the Holy Spirit of God! This is a supernatural work that is accessed by faith in the Name of Jesus Christ.

Observable Indicators: Spiritual Attacker(s)
Child rocks, sucks, bites self: Torment.

Inappropriately aggressive: Rage.

Destructive to others: Violent.

Suffers from sleep and/or speech disorders, Insomnia, mute spirit.

Restricts play activities or experiences: Sadness, depression.

Demonstrates compulsions, obsessions, phobias, Spirit of fear.

Behavioral Indicators in Children
Negative statements about self: Low self-esteem, shame.

Shy, passive, compliant: sadness, depression;

Self-destructive behavior: anger and torment Highly aggressive, hysterical   outbursts: control.

Cruel to others (people or animals): familiar spirit, anger, rage.

Overly demanding: control and manipulation, fear.

In many cases, medication can lessen some of these symptoms or temporarily eliminate them, but complete healing and freedom comes when the child or adult is truly set free by the Power of God through Jesus Christ! The ROOT must be UP-ROOTED!

I am talking about the demonic root of abuse, torment, shame, rejection, sadness, depression, and bipolar symptoms. When these roots are destroyed by and through God's Power there is healing and wholeness. God's Word gives us a perfect example of an immediate uprooting when a man who had been tormented for years ran to Jesus.

"...a man with an impure spirit came from the tombs to meet him. This man lived in the tombs, and no one could bind him anymore, not even with a chain.... No one was strong enough to subdue him. Night and day among the tombs and in the hills, he would cry out and cut himself with stones [he was being attacked by a legion of demonic spirits]. *When he saw Jesus from a distance, he ran and fell on his knees in front of Him. For Jesus had said to him, "Come out of this man, you impure spirit!"*
Mark 5:1-20 (NIV)

~ ~ ~

Depending on the seriousness, the duration, and the sort of abuse, some of those who were abused in their childhood retain certain life-problems due to the trauma. These can be divided into psychological, social, sexual and physical difficulties.

Psychological Problems include: Unreasonable fears, panic attacks, sleeping problems, nightmares, irritability, outbursts of anger and sudden-shock reactions when being touched. People may have little confidence, and self-respect often showing disrespect for one's own body. Behavior that harms the body may develop including addiction to alcohol and other substances, excessive work or involvement in sports, isolating depression, self-destruction (cutting) and prostitution.

Social problems include: Having little trust or confidence in other people, even close family members, resulting in an unreasonable fear of losing relationships, or an exaggerated expectation of being able to control relationships. Also, eating disorders often occur in sexually abused people leading to obesity, anorexia or bulimia,

Among all the effects listed above, there is one common factor that is evident. They are all symptoms or behaviors that mask conscious and/or subconscious traumatic pain.

With the increased number of cases of child abuse over recent years, combined with the countless child pornography and pedophilia cases which have been uncovered, we can clearly see that there are now more abuse victims than we could have ever imagined on this planet. According to many government and health services statistics we know that this is more common than we'd like to believe possible. In surveys of adults, 1 in 4 women and 1 in 6 men report that they were sexually abused as a child. A recent statistic I just read says that every 2 minutes in the United States, someone is sexually abused. It is therefore, most likely that the majority of abuse victims have never shared their stories – continuing to live in pain and torment.

More recently, *Child Help* reported the following National Abuse Statistics of Child Abuse in America. "Children are suffering from a hidden epidemic of abuse and neglect. Every year 3.6 million reports of child abuse are made in the United States involving nearly 6.6 million children (one report can include multiple children). The United States has the worst record in the industrialized nations – losing five children every day due to abuse-related deaths. There is a report of child abuse made every 10 seconds." (Childhelp.org, 2018)

<u>This makes it quite evident that these individual attacks, perpetrated by humans but activated by Satan, are the most powerful weapon he uses to destroy men and women. He</u>

launches the warfare against us as early as possible during childhood, by planting seeds of abuse that grow into weeds of despair, mistrust, and hatred as we grow older. Frequently our childhood experiences are so dark and devastating because the enemy is trying to wipe us out before we can even come to the knowledge of who we are in Christ!

This is not a new tactic. Satan made every attempt to destroy Jesus as soon as He was born, because he knew that our Lord had a mission, a purpose to destroy him and restore us to the Family of God. Matthew 2:16 reads: *Then Herod, when he saw that he was deceived by the wise men, was exceedingly angry; and he sent forth and put to death all the male children who were in Bethlehem and in all its districts, from two years old and under, according to the time which he had determined from the wise men.*

Satan had been working on King Herod's mind, will and emotions for a long time feeding Herod's despair, mistrust, and hatred. When the time came, He was obsessively determined to kill the baby Jesus before He could grow up and fulfill His purpose! Herod believed the enemy's lie that this child was a threat to his rule and reign as an earthly king.

The enemy's strategy has not changed. He tries to destroy us at birth or most certainly before we can grow into finding our true purpose according to God's original design for our lives. We are a threat to Satan's purpose which is to "steal, kill and destroy" everyone in his path. The ultimate goal of Satan and his minions is to keep us from fulfilling the very purpose for which God created us.

By the time an abused child has become an adult, he or she has been mentally tormented by invisible and continuous bad memories and emotional trauma. Oftentimes, there is sexual dysfunction because of the guilt and shame that remains as a residue of verbal, physical and/or sexual abuse. Recent studies at *Johns Hopkins School of Public Health* show that most sexual abuse victims end up suffering from various forms of mental health issues such as depression and schizophrenia. They are also more susceptible to thoughts of death as the only escape and commit suicide. This sadness is often expressed as shame or guilt—a feeling of having caused the abuse incident(s)—which can remain attached to victims all of their lives. It follows a person like a dark shadow—a trauma we've experienced in our lifetime that remains a part of our day to day existence—like a silent partner that I'm certain we all would like to dismiss. This unresolved guilt and shame definitely fits into Satan's plans for us. But, as we now know, **Jesus has made the way for each of us to escape!**

~ ~ ~

Discovering the following statistical data on abuse in America was astounding to me; and, dear Reader, you certainly do not have to read them! However, if you do, remember this:

"Do not be afraid of them,
For I am with you to deliver you," declares the Lord.
Jeremiah 1:8 (NASB)

If you identify with any of these statistical statements, please contact someone to help you. Know that I've been praying for you—and this moment in your life when you're reading these pages—for many years. **God hears our prayers and makes a way for us to find help and come to Him for healing.**

I am the Way, the Truth and the Life
John 14:6

~ ~ ~

Chapter 8

Child Sexual Abuse Statistics

The prevalence of child sexual abuse is difficult to determine because it is often not reported; experts agree that the incidence is far greater than what is reported to authorities. CSA is also not uniformly defined, so statistics may vary. The statistics below represent some of the research done on child sexual abuse.

The U.S. Department of Health and Human Services' Children's Bureau report: *Child Maltreatment 2010*, found that 9.2% of victimized children were sexually assaulted.

Studies by David Finkelhor, Director of the *Crimes Against Children Research*, show that:

- 1 in 5 girls and 1 in 20 boys is a victim of child sexual abuse;
- Self-report studies show that 20% of adult females and 5-10% of adult males recall a childhood sexual assault or sexual abuse incident;

- During a one-year period in the U.S., 16% of youth ages 14 to 17 had been sexually victimized;
- Over the course of their lifetime, 28% of U.S. youth ages 14 to 17 had been sexually victimized;
- Children are most vulnerable to CSA between the ages of 7 and 13.

"According to a *2003 National Institute of Justice* report, 3 out of 4 adolescents who have been sexually assaulted were victimized by someone they knew well." This statistic further proves that most often the abuser is so close to their victim that the abuse is most often physical, painful, and easy to mask and/or cover up.

"A *Bureau of Justice Statistics* report shows 1.6 % (sixteen out of one thousand) of children between the ages of 12-17 were victims of rape/sexual assault"

"A study conducted in 1986 found that 63% of women who had suffered sexual abuse by a family member also reported a rape or attempted rape after the age of 14. Recent studies in 2000, 2002, and 2005 have all concluded similar results." (victimsofcrime.org, 2018)

This statistic was most profound to me, not only because it was my experience but because it also has a strong spiritual message. The initial abuse that I encountered by a family member, as a child made me vulnerable to more attacks. My spirit and soul had been infiltrated and contaminated by the spirit of abuse. Thus, there was an open wound and portal that remained opened for the enemy to attack me. I was of course not aware of this weakness, when I was raped at the age of 19.

I pray now for mothers, daughters, sons and fathers who have a family member or even you were abused as a child, that there will be no more attacks! No more abuse or rape in Jesus Name! I pray divine protection over you and your family members and friends, in Jesus' Name!

Based on statistics from the *National Crime Victimization Survey*, sexual violence is more prevalent at college, compared to other crimes. The *Rape, Abuse & Incest National Network* which has a large network for resources and data, is the nation's largest anti-sexual violence organization. www.rainn.org, 2018

Sexual violence on campus is pervasive. These are sad, but enlightening, statistics.

- 11.2% of all students experience rape or sexual assault through physical force, violence, or incapacitation (among all graduate and undergraduate students).[2]
- Among graduate and professional students, 8.8% of females and 2.2% of males experience rape or sexual assault through physical force, violence, or incapacitation.[2]
- Among undergraduate students, 23.1% of females and 5.4% of males experience rape or sexual assault through physical force, violence, or incapacitation.[2]
- 4.2% of students have experienced stalking since entering college.[2]

Student or not, college-age adults are at high risk for sexual violence.

- Male college-aged students (18-24) are 78% more likely than non-students of the same age to be a victim of rape or sexual assault.[1]
- Female college-aged students (18-24) are 20% less likely than non-students of the same age to be a victim of rape or sexual assault.

Statistics on Males

"Compared to those with no history of sexual abuse, young males who were sexually abused were five times more likely to cause teen pregnancy, three times more likely to have multiple sexual partners and two times more likely to have unprotected sex," according to the study published online and in the June print issue of the *Journal of Adolescent Health.* *http://victimsofcrime.org/media/reporting-on-child-sexual-abuse/child-sexual-abuse-statistics.*

This statistic is so important, as it clearly uncovers an issue that is still not discussed enough, and that is, untold confessions of boys and men who have been sexually abused. This attack of the enemy is clearly an attack against the family as a whole. Boys and teens who are abused at a young age are clearly more infused with the need for sexual activity, as their souls and bodies have been stimulated to need constant gratification. Therefore, they have more sex, more partners and no protection during sex. The consequences of their abuse takes a painful course that effects many others and can last for a lifetime.

> *I now pray for the men, young and old to find deep comfort and restoration of what has been stolen from you and broken. May God reveal His love to you, today, and every day, showing you that what you felt was hopelessly shattered inside of you can be redeemed. May the LORD'S Grace, and Mercy open your eyes to see who you are in His Eyes. And may His Love shine out through you. In Jesus' Name. Amen.*

~ ~ ~

Who are the Victims?
Breakdown by Gender and Age:
Women

- 1 out of every 6 American women has been the victim of an attempted or completed rape in her lifetime (14.8% completed rape; 2.8% attempted rape).
- 17.7 million American women have been victims of attempted or completed rape.
- 9 of every 10 rape victims were female in 2003.
- Lifetime rate of rape/attempted rape for women by race:
    - All women: 17.6%
    - White women: 17.7%
    - Black women: 18.8%
    - Asian Pacific Islander women: 6.8%
    - American Indian/Alaskan women: 34.1%
    - Mixed race women: 24.4%

Men

- About 3% of American men—or 1 in 33—have experienced an attempted or completed rape in their lifetime.
- In 2003, 1 in every 10 rape victims were male.
- 2.78 million men in the U.S. have been victims of sexual assault or rape.
Children
- 15% of sexual assault and rape victims are under age 12.
- 29% are age 12-17.
- 44% are under age 18.
- 80% are under age 30.
- Ages 12-34 are the highest risk years.
- There are reports of babies as young as 9 months, also being rape victims.

Girls ages 16-19 are 4 times more likely than the general population to be victims of rape, attempted rape, or sexual assault.

- 7% of girls in grades 5-8 and 12% of girls in grades 9-12 said they had been sexually abused.
- 3% of boys, grades 5-8 and 5% of boys in grades 9-12 said they had been sexually abused.
- In 1995, local child protection service agencies identified 126,000 children who were victims of either substantiated or indicated sexual abuse.
- Of these, 75% were girls.
- Nearly 30% of child victims were between the age of 4 and 7.
- 93% of juvenile sexual assault victims know their attacker.
- 34.2% of attackers were family members.
- 58.7% were acquaintances.
- Only 7% of the perpetrators were strangers to the victim.

Again, it is no surprise to me that 58% of attackers are acquaintances. Their proximity and privacy in the homes (schools, churches, or athletic sites, etc.) makes the victims easier prey and the attacks more likely to go unnoticed and too often, unreported. This is an area where families need to be more aware of where their children are and who they're with; and talk with each other more freely about what is really taking place behind closed doors. **The *hush-hush* policy can no longer be the status quo for any family if our children are to be safe and grow up in healthy environments.**

On average during 1992-2001, American Indians age 12 or older experienced an estimated 5,900 rapes or sexual assaults.

- American Indians were twice as likely to experience a rape/sexual assault compared to all races.
- Sexual violence makes up 5% of all violent crime committed against American Indians (about the same as for other races).

So, what are the actual ramifications of this data in terms of collateral damage to the individual?

There is growing documented evidence of the depths of the damage experienced by abuse victims that clearly reveals the harm done is too often irreversible. And the biggest contributing factor is that most abuse victims are not abused by strangers.

Pregnancies Resulting from Rape

- In 2012, 346,830 women were raped.
- According to medical reports, the incidence of pregnancy for one-time unprotected sexual intercourse is 5%.

Long-term Effects of Rape

Victims of sexual assault are:

- 3 times more likely to suffer from depression.
- 4 times more likely to contemplate suicide
- 6 times more likely to suffer from post-traumatic stress disorder (PTSD).
- 13 times more likely to abuse alcohol with all its consequences.
- 26 times more likely to abuse drugs with their serious side-effects.

~ ~ ~

WE MUST REMEMBER: *statistics* are but mere human number calculations illustrating the brokenness of our world. They are the tracks left behind by an enemy who attacks hearts and minds to bring about destruction.

Our way through and toward restoration and freedom is through Jesus, Who offers it freely.

"When justice is done,
it brings joy to the righteous, but terror to evildoers."
Proverbs 21:15 (NIV)

Chapter 9

Wounded in the House of My Friends

As the statistics tell us, only 7% of individuals who are abused are victimized by strangers! This confirms that the majority of perpetrators are neighbors, friends/acquaintances, or relatives. This was true for me, as I believe it is true for many who are reading this today.

"For it is not an enemy who reproaches me;
Then I could bear it.
Nor is it one who hates me who has exalted himself against me;
Then I could hide from him.
But it was you, a man my equal,
My companion and my acquaintance.
We took sweet counsel together, ..."
Psalm 55:12-14 (NIV)

Sadly, one or more people we are most familiar with and those we love are often the same people who cause us the greatest pain. Even as we grow up with them, and learn to love and appreciate their better attributes, we unsuspectingly discover that a violent and wounded abuser lives within them, too. Of course, abuse coming at us from any human being is painful and leaves terrible damage behind. However, it is worse when inflicted by a friend or family member.

The very definition of *family* and *friend* has at its core the implicit promise of fidelity, love, trust, and respect, the promise to never intentionally hurt us and always care about our well being. So, when there is a betrayal of what we believed to be true, an assault (physically, mentally, or emotionally), we are wounded in the very depths of our being. One such act of betrayal actually initiated the beginning of Jesus' torture and death upon the Cross.

"Then Satan entered Judas, called Iscariot, one of the Twelve.

And Judas went to the chief priests and the officers of the temple guard

and discussed with them how he might betray Jesus." Luke 22: 3-4 (NIV)

Oh, yes. Satan, the great deceiver and father of lies was on the scene there, too, just like he is in our world today. Why did God allow this to happen? I believe that Jesus answered this for us as He prepared the disciples to receive the Presence and Power of the Holy Spirit, saying, *"...the prince of this world* [Satan] *now stands condemned."* Jesus had His mission to fulfill—His Kingdom Purpose that had been foretold since the days of Adam and Eve. He would not have attained this victory had He not gone to the Cross, shed His Blood for us, died and rose again. And neither would we be able to attain our personal freedom; our Victory in Jesus.

The current world we live in remains broken and tattered by the many free-will choices people continue to make—including those who choose to listen to the lies of Satan as they abuse, manipulate and betray those who are most vulnerable in their own households or neighborhoods.

We must break our silence! Please stop pretending the abuse isn't happening! Please stop sweeping the truth under the rug of silence! **Confront it! Report it!** Intervene in behalf of another family member who you know is also being abused and go to a safe place.

What might we expect when confronting an abuser? Although I wrote about several things we can anticipate in the two chapters on "Confronting the Enemy," here is a quick refresher:

- Denial. The majority of abusers will deny having committed any such act against anyone, and most certainly not against their family member(s).
- Anger. This reaction is always present. Some abusers may hold it in during the actual confrontation, however, it will burn within them until at some point it explodes. If their abuse has included violence, please be sure you have a trustworthy support person there with you.
- Blame: Hearing the abuser twist what happened to you and turn the blame on you is almost as painful as the actual events. Do your best to be prepared for their words to strike you. If you're working with a therapist or counselor, you may want to use role-playing to strengthen your resolve. There is also a breakthrough element here because once the person starts blaming you—or someone else—they are actually admitting that the abuse happened.
- Calling you "crazy" and other things: Because of the current social environment of "No More," "Me, too," and "Enough," abusers may jump on the fact that a small number of people have reported abuses which did not actually happen. Attempting to turn the tables

and label you "crazy" or saying you're "imagining things," gives them a temporary way to escape the moment of confrontation. Again, having someone you trust with you will support your confidence and discourage name-calling.

It is vital that we stand our ground and speak the truth maintaining as much calm as possible. Keeping a moderated tone of voice will not only help us keep control of our own emotions, but it also lessens the chance that the abuser's reaction will escalate. **Remember, you are taking back the power that this person stole from you.** You are moving out of the position of "victim," and into your place of strength as "conqueror." This is a *cleansing* experience that opens the way for more of God's Light to shine in and through you!

The following Scripture (Ephesians 5: 5-14, NKJV) has always encouraged me, placed the facts in front of me, and given me direction.

"For this you know, that no fornicator, unclean person, nor covetous man, who is an idolater, has any inheritance in the kingdom of Christ and God. Let no one deceive you with empty words, for because of these things the wrath of God comes upon the sons of disobedience. Therefore, do not be partakers with them.

For you were once darkness, but now you are light in the Lord. Walk as children of light (for the fruit of the Spirit is in all goodness, righteousness, and truth), finding out what is acceptable to the Lord. And have no fellowship with the unfruitful works of darkness, but rather expose them. For it is shameful even to speak of those things which are done by them in secret. But all things that are ex-

posed are made manifest by the light, for whatever
makes manifest is light. Therefore, He says:
'Awake, you who sleep,
Arise from the dead,
And Christ will give you light.'"

~ ~ ~

Oftentimes in families, abuse that occurred in older or past generations is never discussed. Everyone may *know* about various incidents and pieces of stories passed down through oral histories, but no one ever brought the deeds done in darkness into the light! Many factors play into this and the enemy of our souls, and the souls of future generations, uses them all against us especially the emotions of pride, guilt and shame. These are the main reasons family secrets remain buried in silence, and those secrets and their roots continue to fester in living family members if we do not break free.

What I've discovered, is that when the truth is told, and the crime exposed, everyone is freed! What was meant to continue destroying the family has been brought into the light. The legacy for future generations it turned away from Satan and his lies and the freedom begins when we turn toward Jesus, accepting His finished work on the Cross of Calvary.

The Apostle Paul—who was once one of the strongest persecutors of the first disciples—understood this freedom and encourages everyone to accept New Life.

There is therefore now no condemnation to those
who are in Christ Jesus, who do not walk according
to the flesh, but according to the Spirit. For the law
of the Spirit of life in Christ Jesus has made me free
from the law of sin and death.
Romans 8: 1-3 (NKJV)

As JESUS released His last breath with the words, "It is finished," He removed every stain of guilt and shame—for all generations—and offers each of us a personal relationship with Him today and into Eternity.

Jesus knows every detail of our lives. Literally, every detail from the number of hairs on our heads and the rhythm of our heartbeats, to every good, bad and ugly event that has ever happened, God was there. And yet He loves us so dearly, treasuring each person, that He came to rescue and restore us and our families.

If you and your family have been a victim of a legacy of abuse of any kind, I am praying for you right now:

> In the Name of Jesus Christ, I destroy the root of abuse that exists in your family line! I bind the spirit of abuse that has existed over your family! I release the healing Presence of God to restore and mend every living family member. As each one begins to experience healing and restoration, your family as a unit will be restored and healed walking with God *"not as unwise men but as wise...understanding the will of the Lord...filled with the Holy Spirit...and always giving thanks"*. Amen.
>
> (Ephesians 5: 15-21)

When families move out of that dark place—that was kept hidden in the past and silenced in the present—they begin to encourage each other to seek God's Wisdom in everything. This may include changing the company they keep and/or the places they went for entertainment. This is the time to search for a church home, one that teaches the Bible in all it fullness, where everyone can enjoy the fellowship of other Jesus followers.

As you allow the Holy Spirit to bless you and your family with His guidance, you'll realize more of the Treasures He has for you.

> *"Praise be to the Lord,*
> *for He has heard my cry for mercy.*

The Lord is my strength and my shield;
my heart trusts in Him, and He helps me.
My heart leaps for joy,
and with my song I praise Him.
The Lord is the strength of His people,
a fortress of salvation for His anointed one.
Save Your people and bless Your inheritance;
be their Shepherd and carry them forever."
Psalm 6: 6-9 (NIV)

Chapter 10

Suppressed Trauma Memories

Suppressed memory, in psychologists' terms, is defined as the "memories unconsciously blocked by an individual due to the high level of stress or trauma contained in that memory."

I once counseled a woman who was concerned about thoughts and memories that seemed to come from nowhere. Her memories consisted of flashes of extremely tormenting encounters in a family member's kitchen, where torturous sexual acts were performed on her. These events took place when she was 5 or 6 years old.

When we suppress bad memories as a survival mechanism, we are unable to process the violation that occurred and therefore cannot communicate what is going on inside of us to ourselves or anyone else. The trauma of the experience was too great to process as a child, so the memory was locked away.

The "survival mode" mechanism that temporarily rescued this woman in her youth was no longer active and, at the age of forty-one her painful memories were surfacing. All of a sudden, flashbacks of violent experiences plagued her and as we worked together she discovered that the abuse she suffered has hindered her all of her life. The vivid recollections became more frequent which brought her to a place of needing to tell someone the truth, and she chose me. I consider this to be a sacred place where the Holy Spirit is actively involved in the healing process.

Once these roots of pain are discovered they can then be uprooted through our faith in God and prayers of deliverance and healing. Her willingness to tell me the truth about what her memories revealed allowed them to be unraveled, and up-rooted—a vital process that leads to true relief and freedom.

When the root is identified it can be destroyed and replaced by the Word of God. This activates His Power to heal and re-store the soul to a healthy place, where it can flourish and thrive—where we can *see* a new *vision* for our lives. Our soul will prosper which, in turn, affects our overall health and well being!

Jesus said: *"I came that they may have and enjoy life, and have it in abundance,* to the full, till it overflows."
John 10:10b (AMPC)

~ ~ ~

Be assured I understand the turmoil in the soul of an abused person—like a raging storm within. I know. I have been there. Yet we have God's excellent promise that tells us...

"Call upon Me [God] *in the day of trouble; I will deliver you, ..."*
Psalm 50: 15

~ ~ ~

What creates our suppressed memories?

When remembering how my personal storms affected me, I often think of the familiar Bible story describing a storm that arose when Jesus and the disciples were crossing to the other side of the lake. I can imagine how the wind and the waves beat against the boat almost tossing everyone into the waters, and the experience definitely filled them with great fear. But Jesus was with them—in the storm-tossed boat—and He was asleep. The men woke Him up and yelled at Him, "Don't you care that we're about to die?"

> *He* [Jesus] *got up, rebuked the wind and said to the waves,*
> *'Quiet! Be still!*
> *Then the wind died down and it was completely calm.*
> Mark 4:39 (NIV)

How many of us have wondered if God wasn't asleep on our boat, totally unaware or even worse, uninterested, in what was happening to us. Satan enjoys every moment that these thoughts invade us, and he uses strategies to continue twisting our emotions in knots.

We need to constantly remind ourselves that Jesus, our Father, and the Holy Spirit are always with us during every storm whether great or small and the plan for our rescue is securely and actively engaged.

> Right now, I pray and decree over your life, dear Reader, that the Lord Jesus Christ, gives you peace in the midst of your internal storm! That you have given your life to Him and are cooperating with His Love that heals and restores you and will make you whole again, in spirit, soul and body. Amen.

Because I believe God is Who He says He is, and that He is exceedingly able to do what He says He can do—loving us with an unquenchable, unconditional Love—I know (beyond the shadow of a doubt) that He will heal you. **Every wound, every bit of *internal bleeding* and *mourning*, every *root* of pain and agony that tosses your life upside-down, will be removed!**

> *"...Jesus told him, 'Don't be afraid; just believe."* Mark 5:36b (NIV)

~ ~ ~

It is important for us to understand that the spiritual aspects of abuse are just as real as the medical and psychological aspects. The Lord showed me that trauma experienced during any form of abuse opens a portal in the mind, body, soul and spirit of the individual. This portal makes the person vulnerable and open to all types of demonic oppression. Satan uses the trauma as an opportunity to bombard the mind and soul of a person with a barrage of devastation and torment, so the victim might be unproductive for the rest of their lives. Only through transformation by the renewing of our minds through the Word of God can deliverance be released as the Spirit of God brings complete wholeness to us.

There is a great example of this deliverance in the Bible which I mentioned earlier in Chapter 7. It is about the man from Gadarene who had been so tormented by Satan's demons that his neighbors chained him to try and control his violent outbursts. This incident is recorded in the book of Mark, Chapter 5, verses 1-15 (NIV).

"They went across the lake to the region of the Gadarenes. When Jesus got out of the boat, a man with an impure spirit came from the tombs to meet him. This man lived in the tombs, and no one could bind him anymore, not even with a chain. For he had often been chained hand and foot, but he tore the chains apart and broke the irons on his feet. No one was strong enough to subdue him. Night and day among the tombs and in the hills he would cry out and cut himself with stones.

When he saw Jesus from a distance, he ran and fell on his knees in front of him. He shouted at the top of his voice, "What do you want with me, Jesus, Son of the Most High God? In God's name don't torture me!" For Jesus had said to him, "Come out of this man, you impure spirit!"

Then Jesus asked him, "What is your name?"

"My name is Legion," he replied, "for we are many." And he begged Jesus again and again not to send them out of the area.

A large herd of pigs was feeding on the nearby hillside. The demons begged Jesus, "Send us among the pigs; allow us to go into them." He gave them permission, and the impure spirits came out and went into the pigs. The herd, about two thousand in number, rushed down the steep bank into the lake and were drowned.

Those tending the pigs ran off and reported this in the town and countryside, and the people went out to see what had happened. When they came to Jesus, they saw the man who had been possessed by the legion of demons, sitting there, dressed and in his right mind; and they were afraid."

How did this man find himself living in a graveyard, cutting himself and completely out of his mind? What could have happened in his life to get him to this point? Although we are not told about his past, I would say that he had experienced much devastation, physical pain, as well as abuse in many other forms. That trauma opened his soul to be infiltrated by tormenting spirits from the enemy, Satan. His pain isolated him and caused him to withdraw from family, friends and society all together. Finally, he finds himself most comfortable—protecting others from the uncontrollable violence—living outdoors in the cold, in a graveyard among the dead.

Though this happened in biblical times, there are people alive today who are surviving among "the tombs". They are in a dead place of suppressed memories, tormented by Satan and unable to function in society. We have all seen such people walking past us in grocery stores, or sitting beside us in church, and did not recognize them. Too often their emotions explode and they take the lives of others and then their own—no longer able to cope with the rage, pain and anger they have lived with on a daily basis.

What fascinates me about this event in Scripture is that this one man had 2,000 evil spirits dwelling in him! (This number is inferred because there were 2,000 pigs that ran off the cliff, and the same number of evil spirits.)

Truly, if we have not reconciled ourselves to God through Jesus Christ, we are "open game", if you will, for Satan to wreak havoc in our souls. I can only imagine what this man may have experienced in his childhood and throughout his life. He was so torn within, that he tore himself on the outside. We see this today when children and teens cut themselves as result of the inner turmoil they feel. They can find no peace.

What happened to this man from Gadarenes was that Jesus Christ literally went to the door of this man's soul and confronted what was eating him alive within. The Power of His Presence and the Word of deliverance that He spoke caused the demons to flee from that tormented man and go into the swine. That same power is available to us today—for anyone who cries out to God with a sincere plea for freedom. They will receive it, in the Name of Jesus Christ!

Yes, psychologist and counselors can identify what is traumatizing a person, but only the Power of God can truly liberate the mind, body and soul through the freedom that Jesus Christ wrought for us when He died and rose again from the grave! He literally goes to the door of a person's soul and confronts what is eating us alive—then commands it to be uprooted out of our spirit, soul and body!

In the Name of Jesus Christ, may you receive this very moment a healthy mind, and by the power of His Spirit may your soul be cleansed and made whole by the blood of Jesus. Amen!

Right now, put this book down for a moment and lift your hands high. Tell God this: Lord, I receive

Your healing for my mind, body and soul! Cleanse my spirit by the Power of Your Spirit from any and all torments of Satan, and the pain and trauma that he placed upon me. Stop my soul from this *internally bleeding*! In Jesus name! Amen!

~ ~ ~

Rape Is A Major Cause of Suppressed Memories

Scripture gives us this definition of rape:

> *"But if out in the country a man happens to meet a young woman pledged to be married and rapes her, only the man who has done this shall die. Do nothing to the woman; she has committed no sin deserving death. This case is like that of someone who attacks and murders a neighbor, for the man found the young woman out in the country, and though the betrothed woman screamed, there was no one to rescue her."*
>
> Deuteronomy 22: 25-27 (NIV)

After "No," it's rape!

I experienced the loss of my virginity through date-rape. Not only did I feel physical pain, but I knew that my perpetrator was robbing me of something precious that God had given me. I did not realize the extent of the trauma that this experience caused me until I got married at the age of 21 and found myself completely unable to enjoy sexual relations with my husband. Thank God, through Jesus Christ, that at this juncture I realized that I would have to allow the Lord to take me through a healing process, so that I could completely recover from that rape experience. He did just that, and during that time He gave me the outline for this book to help others go through their process of healing and restoration, with Him.

One of the biggest obstacles that blocks this process is our unwillingness to speak the truth about the rape to ourselves and especially to others. A sin (and a crime) has been committed that we did not willingly participate in; we were forced! We were a victim. Just as the woman in the Scripture above, we did no wrong.

Under the Old Testament Law, the rapist was to be sentenced to death. However, in our present time, many perpetrators go free because the victims remain silent. Though you may never have shared your experiences with anyone, it is important now that you talk to God about what happened and begin to open up your heart so that your healing process can begin. The hard part is revealing the truth of the assault, and if known, eventually confronting the rapist.

The Word of God also says that when you have found the thief, he must return to you seven-times what he had stolen. I must say that despite the deep pain and trauma we have experienced in our lives, when the thief (abuser, rapist) is found, and we receive our healing, everything they stole from us is restored in so many ways. **I want to encourage you and let you know that God restores us in incredible ways that we could not anticipate. Our restoration brings to us the peace and joy and love that we rightfully deserve.**

"Yet if he is caught, he must pay sevenfold,
though it costs him all the wealth of his house."
Proverbs 6:31 (NIV)

My prayer for you at this moment is this...

Dear Father God, I present to you this dear soul who has suffered the experience of rape. Standing with them in prayer today, together we ask You to lift this attack off their hearts, minds and bodies. Remove every touch of the perpetrator's spirit and cleanse them of all defilement. Replace those moments with Your Love and send the Holy Spirit to bring complete healing. In Jesus' Name we pray. Amen.

Surely He took up our pain
and bore our suffering, ...

...and by His wounds we are healed.
Isaiah 53: 4-5 (NIV)

~ ~ ~

A Vicious Cycle In A Private Prison

There is another category of rape that is even more rarely reported, and it occurs within a marriage—the place we are supposed to be safest. Once the enemy deceives a spouse to believe that the inhumane, evil way they treat their partner is necessary and acceptable, a vicious cycle begins. After years of abuse, apologies, forgiveness, seeming improvement and then more abuse, a woman or man can become emotionally numb, complacent and accepting of the situation. In most cases, there is an intense fear that keeps the person trapped and immobilized. Fear that if they tell anyone or try to escape, the abuse will be even harsher. And if they actually leave the marriage, the physical punishment will be greater. The cage (the front door) may open but the bird (the abused spouse) has no wings to fly out and seemingly chooses to remain trapped in a bad and dangerous situation.

The spirit of fear is one of Satan's powerful tools that can cause a person to completely shut down and ignore their own torment; internally and externally. However, it is not more powerful than God and His rescue plan. He does not want us to be trapped in this unhealthy place, nor does He want the physical and emotional damage spilling over onto others in the family. With great compassion He will lead the victim(s) out—if they cooperate.

There is no fear in love; but perfect love casts out fear, because fear involves torment.
But he who fears has not been made perfect in love.
1 John 4:18 (NKJV)

If you are imprisoned in such a relationship—functioning in constant survival mode—going to work, taking care of the children and barely taking care of yourself, you may believe that you must stay for the sake of the children and/or for financial security. This is also a ploy of the enemy, leading victims into denial, so that they refuse to believe or recognize the truth that the person they "love" is abusing them. If stuck in this way of coping for too long, people may withdraw from their normal social activities or any emotional involvement at all.

No place in this survival mode cycle is a good place. It is time for you to break free! All of these symptoms and circumstances create a downward spiral of pain, torment and turmoil that only the delivering power of God can break. **The Lord is more than able to break the cycle and give you His peace and total freedom from all bondage!**

I recently counseled a woman who was in such a situation. Every day she experienced physical, verbal and emotional abuse. Fear had gripped her so tightly that she was unable to think clearly, and sincerely believed that she was trapped because of the lack of finances and could never leave her husband for fear of what he might do to her if she did leave.

Now, a year later—after extensive prayer and counseling—she has found a safe place to heal, get on her feet, and rebuild her life. She can now see the devastation and damage that was done to her heart and mind, staying in a bad place for so long! She was *bleeding internally,* and *mourning* the relationship that could have been. She almost lost her mind before escaping her prison of abuse. Interestingly enough, as the Lord moved her along the healing process, we learned that this woman is called to pastor a church. She has great God-given purpose and destiny inside of herself that must be fulfilled, as we all do.

And the God of all grace, who called you to His eternal glory in Christ,
after you have suffered a little while, will Himself restore you and make you strong, firm and steadfast.
1Peter 5:10 (NIV).

<u>You may not believe this, but sometimes our suffering is allowed on purpose for a purpose. God permits devastation in our lives so that we will find our way to Him and through the process, and have a testimony to share. We become the proof—the evidence—that we survived heart-wrenching and painful experiences and lived to talk about it, just like Jesus did.</u>

My husband always says our experiences in life, and relationships with people, are either a blessing or a lesson. Based on all the trauma that many of us have endured, we have learned many lessons that have developed strong character within us and brought us into our personal relationship with God, Himself.

He has promised us in His Word that after the suffering and pain, He will strengthen, establish and perfect us! Our suffering in not in vain nor does last forever. God has declared that He will make everything beautiful in its time (Ecclesiastes 3:11). Please allow me to pray with you now, for complete healing within you and your family.

Dear Lord, Jesus, thank You for rescuing these Readers and showing them the way to You. Today, we need Your Grace to be able to forgive those in our families who have hurt and abused us. Please heal us of all the traumatic experiences so that we might receive Your Peace, Healing and Restoration. Surround us in Your Light, Lord, so that the plans of the enemy are revealed and our *mourning* and *internal bleeding* stops! Thank You for being our Saving Grace. Amen.

~ ~ ~

I was recently blessed to hear a message given by a young Pastor in Colorado. He spoke about the Ascension of Jesus with such inspiration that I must share my summary of it here, because it reveals how much Jesus loves us and wants to supernaturally heal our most traumatic experiences while giving us new vision for our futures.

As you might understand, Jesus' followers had witnessed the events of His abuse at the hands of the Roman soldiers. They saw the crown of thorns tearing His scalp and the scourging that ripped the flesh from His back; they saw the nails piercing His hands and feet; and heard His last breath as it escaped cracked and bleeding lips. And His death filled them with fear—fear that this would be their fate, too.

Although most of us have not been part of a family that experienced such extreme trauma, many of us have survived terrible abuse within our family/friend associations—abuse that shut us down and imprisoned us. The disciples were also physically, mentally, emotionally and spiritually shut down. All their hopes and dreams for the future seemed *dead*.

By the time Jesus' Ascension into Heaven came, He had been physically walking with and teaching His followers for many days, *"...to whom He presented Himself alive after His suffering by many infallible proofs, ..."* (Acts 1:3 NKJV). On that Ascension Day Jesus was, quite literally, standing with both of His feet on the ground with them, and *"...while they watched, He was taken up, and a cloud received Him out of their sight."* (vs 9)

This moment—this "sight"—refocused their hearts toward the future. In His great love for those men and women, and all of us today, Jesus *healed* their traumatic memories of His death upon the Cross! Yes, they remembered the Work of the Cross that made the Way for us to receive Jesus as our Savior/ Redeemer. **However, their distressing, fearful memories were healed; their purpose and focus was reset with a more complete understanding of the Glory of God and His Supernatural plan to return!**

"And while they looked steadfastly toward heaven as He went up, behold, two men stood by them in

white apparel, who also said, 'Men of Galilee, why do you stand gazing up into heaven? This same Jesus, who was taken up from you into heaven, will so come in like manner as you saw Him go into heaven.'"
(verse 10-11)

My friends, there is no Greater Love that exists! Jesus does not want any of us to experience abuse. But when our broken world cooperates with Satan to harm the innocent, they will face God's Justice, and we will experience His Healing!

Chapter 11

Destroying Every Yoke

The Word of the Lord says,
*"It shall come to pass in that day
that his burden will be taken away from your shoulder,
and his yoke from your neck,
and the yoke shall be destroyed because of the anointing
oil."*
Isaiah 10:27 (NKJV)

As mentioned earlier, there are certain tormenting spirits that must be bound in prayer so that every stronghold is destroyed in your life. Let's look closer at this Scripture to glean the comparison between the days of Isaiah and our present situations.

I believe that as you pray the prayers given to you in this book, the Presence of God will draw near to you and He will uproot your enemy, Satan, and cast out all oppressive forces, destroying them by His Almighty Power!

The burden that you have been carrying for some time now is weighty, painful and suffocating. This is much like the iron shackle *yoke* that is placed around the neck of an animal, such as an ox, to bind him to his task and keep him in position—in his place. This Scripture historically speaks of the bondage and slavery of the children of Israel. Unless their "owners" were compassionate people, the shackles they wore could bruise wrists and ankles or tear flesh. And these *yokes* definitely kept them in their place—in fear and bondage.

It is the same in the spiritual sense. The yokes of spiritual bondage are demonic strongholds that chokes the life out of a person, hinders progress and the ability to hear God, to see God and live in the freedom He provides for us. Therefore, the spiritual yokes/burdens we experience are the attacks of Satan placing on us the weight of fear, anxiety, and loss of freedom.

But God has other plans for us. "*The yoke shall be destroyed because of the anointing oil!*" In the days of Isaiah, when oil was poured over the neck of an ox, his shackles were easily removed. So it will be when God's supernatural anointing oil is poured into our lives. His Power and Grace dispels and destroys the shackles of bondage in our lives!

I decree and declare to you this very moment that the yoke of bondage and abuse is destroyed in your life! In the name of Jesus Christ! The yoke is shattered and broken into pieces. You are free to be who God has called and destined you to be. Lift your hands right now and praise God for freedom! *"Who the Son sets free is free indeed!"* (John 8:36)

~ ~ ~

There is a song titled, *I Can See Clearly Now*, written by Johnny Nash in 1972. The song speaks of how after the rain everything is so much clearer and there is hope now that the sun is shining again. I believe this inspirational song reflects the feeling of freedom and peace Nash experienced after his pain and burdens were lifted from his shoulders by the Power and Grace of God. We, too, can experience this same freedom and live again without fear and sadness.

~ ~ ~

Unable to speak. Unable to feel. Unable to Function.

These are the symptoms—the results—of the devastating trauma of abuse you have experienced when your emotions were shattered, and you are imprisoned by pain. However, God tells us in His Word that...

"...He will wipe away every tear from their eyes,
and there will no longer be any death;
there will no longer be any mourning, or crying, or pain;
the first things have passed away
Revelations 21:4 (NASB)

It is not by accident that you are reading this book, and right now you feel a little better than you did before you started. As you have been reading and praying you may have already noticed that your *internal bleeding* and *mourning* has stopped; that some of the *roots* of depression, fear and anxiety are being pulled up! WOW! I am so thankful to God for what He's doing in your life!

Even so, you may still feel like you are not important to anyone on this planet and that no one (even the people in your immediate family) cares about you or what happens to you in your life. Therefore, it is up to you to remember that God, the Creator of the ALL things, does care about you immensely! He cares about every detail of your life-story and actually has a unique and marvelous plan for your life.

The Lord sees our wounds. He knows that like any type of external wound, when treated with the proper medicine (ice, heat or antibiotic balm), healing begins. We are like those with physical open wounds, who need treatment and time to heal from the internal and spiritual trauma we have been walking around with for so long. Many of us have never dared to hope to feel better, let alone receive the Tender Loving Care that God offers. Often this healing is a process, and for some it is an earthly lifetime process as we begin to walk in God's plan to reach out and help others find their way to restoration and peace.

Feeling the way you've felt, can you even imagine helping others find freedom from their abuse trauma? You can! This happens as we follow Jesus and His Ways.

"Jesus looked at them and said, 'With man this is impossible, but with God all things are possible'"
(Matthew 19:26)

~ ~ ~

Destroying Soul-Ties/Deadly Roots

When we embrace and hold someone closely to us, sharing with them in physical intimacy—whether with or without our permission—their souls are tied to us and their spirits become a part of us. We take on the characteristics of what we are embracing.

Can a man take fire in his bosom
And his clothes not be burned?
So is the one who goes in to his neighbor's wife;
Whoever touches her will not go unpunished.
Proverbs 6: 27 & 28 (NASB)
In the transgression of an evil man there is a snare:...
Proverbs 29:6a

What this Scripture tells us is that when we embrace another person and take them into our heart, body and soul, we are *snared*, trapped, apprehended, and become consumed by whatever consumes them. It is either Light or darkness; Godly or ungodly; death or life. Any snare that captured us as the result of an ungodly soul tie, will be an evil spirit that enters into our life and immediately begins to torment us.

As I shared earlier, the ungodly soul-ties that snared me when I was raped in college, hindered my relationship with my future husband. Even though I was totally unaware of this at first, those evil spirits kept us from properly bonding as husband and wife, which was part of what led to our eventual divorce. We must remember that marriage is so much more than a piece of paper, a beautiful cake, and wedding rings. Marriage is a covenant relationship between the man and the woman with God. It is vital to your relationship that all ungodly soul-ties are broken, destroyed in the Name of Jesus, including any from previous relationships that you might have been deceived into believing were "healthy relationships."

Also mentioned in the previous chapter is the abusive marriage. Time and again crisis counselors, and police see the abused person return to that marriage. This is where the soul-ties come into play and we can actually become comfortable being *tied* to that which is unclean because it has now latched on to our spirit. These are evil spirit soul-ties that bind us together with the perpetrator of our pain. It may be invisible to the eye, but it is as real as a coil of steel. Until the soul-ties are broken, and the evil spirits are uprooted and destroyed, the torment and abuse will continue because they have contaminated us in flesh and spirit.

Long after we are no longer associated with that person, soul-ties can remain. Every bondage and sin—every act of cooperation with Satan and his demons—that we have experienced is fused within our soul and we carry that burden and struggle, along with your own, everywhere we go.

This is quite a load to bear, but we all have been guilty of this and walked in the darkness of soul-ties, believing that the momentary pleasures between the abusive pain, was worth the cost, being deceived into not realizing the damage that was being done.

Arriving at the truth about the bondage of soul-ties is a big step toward allowing God to free us, break every soul-tie-root, and heal us, replacing it all with His Peace.

I pray now, in the Name of Jesus, that every soul tie in your life be destroyed! Every unclean snare and connection that contaminated your soul and spirit is now uprooted and you are free and cleansed through and by the Blood of Jesus! AMEN!!

"Bless the Lord, O my soul,
And forget not all His benefits:
Who forgives all your iniquities,
Who heals all your diseases,
Who redeems your life from destruction,
Who crowns you with lovingkindness and tender mercies,..."
Psalm 103:2-4 (NKJV)

Please pray this prayer out loud!

Father, in the name of Jesus, I thank You that I survived my experience(s) of abuse. I now know that it is Your desire that I not be just a survivor, but to be totally free from all the damage done to my heart, soul and mind. I ask You now to remove the very roots of abuse in my soul; along with the rejection, confusion, shame, sadness, fear and torment that have ravaged my soul. In Jesus' Name, I am now free from all bondage and decree that I am restored to my relationship with You, Father; the intimate relationship that You have always intended for my life, through and by the Blood of Jesus Christ! From this day forward, Father God, may my only soul-tie be with You. Amen.

Chapter 12

Healed In Relationships By the WORD of God

Once we have been deeply wounded by others, the normal human reaction is to isolate ourselves from people all together to avoid more hurt. However, the opposite reaction can also happen, and we become reckless and enter relationships with the wrong people who are out of control and allow us to be out of control too. While this may feel like fun for a short time, we end up getting wounded even more. Restoration of the whole person must take place before we can truly have healthy relationships with ourselves and with others.

For all of our abused lives, our inability to face our pain and find the path to freedom has caused our relationships with others to be twisted and warped. Our self-image is greatly distorted when we are *bleeding* inside. Therefore, our ability to have healthy relationships in life is extremely limited. People observe us from the outside and have no idea that our view of ourselves is distorted and clouded by what's destroying us on the inside.

I have seen people who have such a negative view of themselves that they must put on a masque of behavior that is almost believable. However, when we hear them talk, or look into their eyes and see their heart, we immediately see their hurt. Victims of abuse are unable to see how they really look because their viewpoint and opinion of themselves is damaged and skewed by the wounds they carry daily—wounds that have never healed. When they look into a mirror, it is cracked and reflects a distorted image. They do not see themselves in the image of God. They have incredible potential and people tell them how beautiful and smart they are; however, they cannot see or believe what others see.

~ ~ ~

Now, I ask you to go a little deeper for a moment and complete this exercise.
Find a mirror and take a look at yourself.

Chapter 13

Look in the Mirror

On the lines below write down what you see in the mirror and you define your reflection:

_____

_____

_____

_____

_____

_____

_____.

When any person is abused, and the *internal bleeding* begins, we lose perspective. We can only *see* ourselves through the lens of the abuser and the hateful remarks they throw at us. And, we have no real strength or ability to have a healthy relationship with anyone because of the soul-ties. **The Lord can restore us in all these areas and thereby redevelop our abilities to acquire and maintain good relationships as He makes us whole from the inside out.**

Part of overcoming this inner battle is through sharing our struggle—and victories—with loved ones. This may not be possible at first, but everyone needs to find out what works best for them. One person may be more comfortable talking to a counselor. Another may prefer talking with a minister in a private setting where we can receive personal deliverance as we lay everything down at the Cross of Christ.

Whatever way someone selects, it is important to move out of isolation so that we don't become entangled again in the pain that God is liberating us from. Ask Him right now to heal your self-image. For we were made in the image and likeness of God our Creator! Every Scripture brings life to us! The Word of God Heals Us!

I will praise You, for I am fearfully and wonderfully made;
Marvelous are Your works,
And that my soul knows very well.
Psalms 139: 14 (NKJV)

~ ~ ~

Chapter 14

"He was wounded for our transgressions,
He was bruised for our iniquities,
the chastisement of our peace was upon Him
and with His stripes we are healed."
Isaiah: 53:4-5 (KJV)

I shared this Scripture in an earlier chapter; however, I also placed it here so that we might take a stronger hold of it and make it personal. The Prophet Isaiah was revealing to the people that Jesus, the living, breathing Word of God, would freely offer Himself (in human form) to rescue us; that Jesus would be wounded for MY transgressions and bruised for MY iniquities; that the "chastisement" or punishment placed upon Him (instead of me) would bring me peace—release me from a punishment that my sins deserve, but that I could not endure. Yet, Jesus endured the sorrows (my sins), whatever they were, which was needful to secure our peace with God. This is, indeed, transforming and life giving! His sacrifice FOR ME has healed me and made me whole!!!

This great miracle makes our healing complete, yet we have to put our faith in action to receive it from Him. It's as if we are reaching out our hands to be rescued by a Hand that is bigger than our own! The act of reaching is our faith in what we cannot see is there! Yet, we can quite literally grasp hold of it, if we believe!

It is important to understand that the Word of God is alive and full of power! The Word of God is the voice of God. There is life and restoration in the Word of God!

> *"For the Word of God is living and powerful, and sharper than any two-edged sword, piercing even to the division of soul and spirit, and of joints and marrow, and is a discerner of the thoughts and intents of the heart. And there is no creature hidden from His sight, but all things are naked and open to the eyes of Him to Whom we must give account."* Hebrews 4:12-13 (NKJV)

The last portion of this Scripture tells us that God is here with us and has always been here. He knew what happened to us, because He was there, and nothing is hidden from His sight. He saw it all. He saw those who took advantage of our vulnerability. He saw our bad choices. It was all "naked and open to His eyes."

The Word (Scripture) *uncovers* us so God can begin to repair us. When we hear It or read It and seek to understand and receive It, we are uncovered. It finds us right where we are, and brings correction, affirmation, revelation, liberty and most of all the Truth.

The Word of God is alive and It "pierces" our soul and divides it! This is a different type of surgical experience for sure, dividing sin from a healthy relationship with God. The Word of God shows us what really is in our heart and brings it to the surface so that we can repent, forgive others, seek forgiveness, and be healed.

It teaches us that Jesus Christ was wounded so that our wounds could be healed. He bled and died for us so that all our *internal bleeding* could stop. Receive it now in your spirit with confidence that God loves you and, at this very moment, you are being completely healed of every harsh word spoken, every unwelcomed sexual experience, every beating and abuse.

You are healed in the matchless Name of Jesus Christ! May His presence overshadow you now and give you peace as He takes away all the pain, hurt, rejection and residue resulting from your trauma. Deliverance is here for you right now. Receive God's Love and know your pain has ended. Tears may fall, but you will begin to feel lighter as the Presence of God surrounds and fills you!

~ ~ ~

I remember an incredible personal encounter I had with God. I was lying on my bed and I sensed the Presence of the Lord in the room. The Spirit of God spoke to me so clearly, "I am going to give you a brand-new heart". In the Spirit I could see a hand reaching into my chest and pulling out a beaten, worn out, crushed heart that was beyond repair. Then I saw another hand put in a brand-new heart. **The old heart had been so worn out by rejection and abuse that it had lost all ability to feel. With my new heart I was made whole.**

The Scripture that comes to mind as I recall this moment is...

"Create in me a clean heart, O God; and renew a right spirit within me."

Psalm 51:10. (KJV)

This *clean heart* is not just a cleansing from sin (which we need) but a removal of pain, *internal bleeding, mourning* and the *roots* that choked us! No surgeon can do this work. It is done by the Spirit of God cleansing and renewing your spirit within.

Another confirming Scripture for me speaks to the work of the Great Physician

replacing the broken heart with the new and clean heart by God's Surgeon Hands.

Jeremiah 8: 22 (KJV) says:

"Is there no balm in Gilead; is there no physician there?

why then is not the health of the daughter of my people recovered?"

Balm is a healing agent, a salve, if you will. Gilead was a mountainous land where the leaves of the balsam tree provided a fragrant oil with healing properties in its leaves.

The definition of the *Balm of Gilead* from the Webster's Dictionary is:

1. an agency that soothes, relieves, or heals
2. a small evergreen African and Asian tree with aromatic leaves; also: a fragrant oleoresin from this tree
3. any of several poplars having resinous buds: as a hybrid North American tree with broadly ornate leaves that are pubescent especially on the underside.

Symbolically, Jesus Christ is the Balm in Gilead. He gave His life for our salvation and healing. His total, unconditional love is like a medicine that heals wounded hearts and spirits!

"Then they cried out to the LORD in their trouble,
and He saved them out of their distresses.
He sent His Word, and healed them,
and delivered them from their destructions."
Psalm 107: 19-20 (NKJV)

Please Pray this prayer:

Father in the Name of Jesus, I open my wounded heart, mind, body and spirit and ask You to heal me completely! Thank You for Your relief, comfort and peace in exchange for my torment, anguish, depression and trauma. Let the fragrance and sweetness of Your love blow over my heart and soul like a fresh wind; like a good medicine for all my wounds. I thank You for total healing from heartache and bad memories! I receive and accept my healing and I am whole! Amen!

The Word of God, His Words written in the Bible are, in and of themselves, healing to our souls! As you have been reading this book, the Power of the Word of God in the scriptures shared, have been touching your spirit and healing you! Know this, whenever you cry out to God, He hears you! **He wants to deliver you! He wants to totally heal you!**

Chapter 15

FREE AT LAST!

"Weeping may endure for a night, but joy comes in the morning."
Psalm 30:5b (NKJV)

After a long time of mourning and being under a dark cloud of despair, joy really does come. The Spirit of the Living God restores, renews and ignites that dead place in us and we can actually laugh, smile and live again.

God loves to bring
that which is dead
back to life!
Death, hell and the grave were all defeated,
just for you!

To be really, truly free is priceless. Jesus Christ paid for your freedom with His suffering on the Cross and when He rose again from the dead. The chains that were binding you; the soul-tie traumas, lies and deceits, have been broken forever!

When you look at the world around you; the grass growing, the brilliant blue sky and cloud formations, and hear the many species of birds singing—you can see the colors and hear the sounds with a new clarity. Your spirit has been set free by the

Chief Liberator, Jesus Christ, the Author and Finisher of our faith!

When the enemy set out to destroy you, he rolled a stone over you (many stones) and pushed you into a grave. Everyone thought you would remain in this dead place. They thought that you would never be healed, never be the functional, strong, wife or mother—husband or father—that you were intended to be. Today, the Lord is opening up your tomb and bidding you to "Come forth out of your grave!"

In the Bible's New Testament, we are told about the event when Jesus's close friend Lazarus became very ill and Jesus did not get to his house before he died. In Jesus' times and even still today, bodies are wrapped in grave clothes to protect and seal the body prior to being placed in the tomb. So, not only must we come out of the tomb, but once out, we must be liberated from our grave clothes! This is the Scripture I'm referring to:

"Now Martha said to Jesus, 'Lord, if You had been here, my brother would not have died. But even now I know that whatever You ask of God, God will give You.' Jesus said to her, 'Your brother will rise again.' Martha said to Him, 'I know that he will rise again in the resurrection at the last day.' Jesus said to her, 'I am the resurrection and the life. He who believes in Me, though he may die, he shall live. And whoever lives and believes in Me shall never die. Do you believe this?' She said to Him, 'Yes, Lord, I believe that You are the Christ, the Son of God, Who is to come into the world.' John 11:21-27 (NKJV)

~ ~ ~

Like me, you may have asked the question, why we were abused? Why did God allow it? Just as Martha and Mary asked Jesus, why He couldn't have come before their brother died. I have come to understand that the *Glory* God receives in these moments of restoration (and the continuing testimonies) brings many more to Life Everlasting than if the circumstances had never occurred. The miracle of bringing Lazarus back to life—and bringing us back to life after suffering the trauma of abuse—speaks to thousands, millions, even billions of people throughout this and future generations. It also brings *transformation* not just for the one individual who was raised, but for many!

Because of Jesus Christ, I arose one day and never looked back. I learned to love again, laugh again, discover the beauty of each new day wrapped in His Mercy, Grace, and Wisdom. God's love healed and restored me to be a whole person; spirit, soul and body!

> *"Now when He had said these things, He cried with a loud voice, 'Lazarus, come forth!' And he who had died came out bound hand and foot with graveclothes, and his face was wrapped with a cloth. Jesus said to them, 'Loose him, and let him go.'"*

John 11: 43-44 (NKJV)

Long ago I wondered why Jesus left his friend bound in grave clothes as he came out of the tomb. He had just healed Lazarus—brought him back from the dead! Then a few moments later Jesus told the relatives and friends, and others gathered for the funeral, to *"Loose him, and let him go."*

Sometime later, as I allowed the Holy Spirit to speak into my life at deeper levels, I learned the symbolic meaning of those pieces of cloth, and Jesus' direction to the people who were present—mourners.

Many had come to comfort and care for Lazarus' sisters, Mary and Martha, and they were grieving, too; in *mourning* over the friendship and relationship that was lost. But when Jesus told them to remove the clothes from the now-living Lazarus, He was placing them in position to care for and support Lazarus in his "new" life—just like He does for us, today. Whether we're aware of it or not, He has placed people in position in our lives to be our support as we go through His healing process.

The clothes were designed to preserve a body while in the tomb—to keep it from falling apart during decay. For us, they represent the shedding of what was holding us in bondage often causing us to feel dead inside because of the trauma of abuse.

But NOW we can be Free at Last! Jesus, The Living Word, has spoken to us to *"Come Forth"* and allow Him to remove the old memories of the pain of *internal bleeding* and the grief of *mourning* that kept us in bound. Once we are lifted and resurrected from our "dead place" we no longer need those clothes! We will no longer fall apart! Alleluia!

The Lord, Jesus, is speaking to you right now through His Word! He is calling to Sarah, Marie, Deborah, Joan, Susan, Evelyn, Lauren; Maggie, Simone, Pearl, Michael, Emma, Barbara, Jeff, Celeste, David, Ina, Marva, Casey, Anna, and Rachel, and (add your name here); **COME FORTH!**

I speak to the grave clothes that have you bound and say, "Be loosed and set free by the power of God, in the Name of Jesus!" Lift your hands just for a moment and tell God, "Thank You for loving me. Thank You for this moment."

May His Presence now engulf you in the place where you are today.

~ ~ ~

One of the most precious and widely read Psalms in the Bible is the 23rd Psalm. It speaks to the heart of the Lord toward us as the Shepherd who nurtures, cares for, and protects us—His sheep. I've added my personal application of this Psalm here so that through it you, too, might seek the Lord, Jesus as the Shepherd of your life.

Psalm 23 (RVS)

1. *"The LORD is my Shepherd, I shall not want."*

The Lord, the One to whom I now surrender my entire life, is my Covering, my Keeper, and my Protector. There is absolutely nothing I need that He cannot provide. He sends the answers before I can open my mouth to speak. He is my blanket of security over me. He is everything I need and more.

2. *"He makes me lie down in green pastures; He leads me beside the still waters."*

He ushers me into a rest that lulls every fiber of my being to BE STILL and rest on a fresh field of green where the sun always shines. It is a supernatural encounter in a place where the Lord, Himself, is the living water there and I can drink of Him and thereafter never thirst.

3. *"He restores my soul. He leads me in paths of righteousness for His name's sake."*

The Lord gives me back everything that was stripped away and stolen from me. With His restorative power He gives me more than I had; more grace, more love, more peace and more strength to be who He called me to be when He created me! He shows me His ways by drawing me closer to Himself through His love. My desire to know more about Him grows and grows, and I open the Bible/Scripture, His Word, discovering the promises that are mine – if I just believe in them through the power of His name.

4. *"Even though I walk through the valley of the shadow of death, I fear no evil; for You are with me;"*

Even in the hardest of times, when I absolutely felt deserted, devastated and rejected, and everyone turned their back on me, the Lord was there! Everything in my life died; people, relationships and my desire to exist began to diminish. But the Lord gave me Hope and caused me to not be afraid. Despite it all, I could still feel His presence, so I was able to finally lift my head once again and smile.

5 **"Thy rod and Thy staff, they comfort me.**

A shepherd's rod and staff were his tools to protect his sheep from marauders and wild animals, and also for discipline. The image given to us here—of the shepherd in the open, rocky field, with danger abounding—makes it clear that leaving The Shepherd's side is a serious mistake. It is His desire to comfort us with His unconditional and unfailing love, mercy and grace. As my fellowship with the Lord grows I receive more of His strength and become aware of His protection on so many levels.

6. Thou preparest a table before me in the presence of my enemies; Thou anointest my head with oil; my cup overflows.

In the face of all of those who thought I was down for the count, and that I would never fulfill my purpose in life (even some who really wanted me to fail), You, Lord, have crowned me, and robed me in Your Glory. You have prepared a feast of elegance on Your best china and made me a name and a praise to Your Glory in the earth and in the face of my enemies. You poured the fresh oil of Your Spirit upon my head and filled me with the power of Your presence. I am now completely renewed, restored and released to soar on the wings of an eagle.

7. Surely goodness and mercy shall follow me all the days of my life; and I shall dwell in the house of the LORD forever.

Truly all the days of my life on this earth and beyond, Your Glory, Lord—Your Goodness and Mercy shall fill me and cover me. I am now part of Your eternal purpose to assist in Your Kingdom coming to earth. I will forever dwell in Your house abiding in the fullness of Your presence. I will serve You today and for all eternity, for You are the God of all creation; You are my Heavenly Father and I am Your child.

Chapter 16

Wounded Healers

I would be remiss, and this may sound like a contradiction—but I must make mention of the many pastors, leaders, ministers and counselors I've met in my 37 years in the ministry; men and women who have a calling and a heart to minister to others and yet continue to suffer from the trauma of abuse, seemingly not able to find healing for themselves. We all go through struggles as we grow in our faith—as the Apostle Paul wrote about. However, at times, we feel stuck in a place of pain (the *internal bleeding* from abuse) and feel powerless to stand up under the weight of it. We know that our God is The Deliverer, yet we remain bound. We have seen Him heal others through our own prayers for them, yet we continue to suffer.

Why? It is because we have not yet received the healing balm that is readily available to us. We have buried our pain behind our ministry, church, and family. We keep ourselves busy with church work and family so that we don't have to deal with the real roots of hurt, rejection and abuse that eats away at us every day.

Unfortunately, with all good intentions and service to family and ministry, we can also *bleed* on everyone we meet! We unintentionally inflict our own pain and hurt upon the ones

we are trying to help. And, when we forget that we need ministry ourselves, we subconsciously avoid getting help! Yet,
those around us see our pain despite the mask that we wear.
**It's time—past time—to live the abundant life that is right-
fully ours! It is vital that ministers be ministered to, so they
are whole and healthy to minister to the needs of others.**

I believe we must come to a time and place where the *internal bleeding* of every abused and traumatized ministers stops;
where they, too, are completely healed and whole!

If you are a minister, pastor, priest, elder or carry the calling
of ministry, this is your moment to call upon the name of the
Lord your God and cry out for your freedom. Let's stop and
pray right now!

Pray this prayer out loud:

> In my distress, I call to You, Lord, I cry out to my
> God for help. From Your Temple You hear my voice;
> my cry comes before Your ears. You reach down
> from on high and take hold of me; You are draw-
> ing me out of deep waters and healing my wounded
> spirit.
>
> (Psalm 18:6 and 16)

~ ~ ~

There has always been a full-on attack against leadership in
the church meant to divide us and make our message of the
Lord's Kingdom ineffective. Satan, indeed, seeks to kill and destroy us. It seems that throughout history, and certainly in our
current day, the devil and his minions succeed too often—sab-
otaging us individually and creating chasms between church
leaders.

One of the most abuse-driven attacks against us is the *spirit
of depression* which too often leads to suicide. Oh, how pleased
Satan is when a minister takes his own life before God's plans
for and within that person are complete. Oh, how his minions
laugh when those closest to that minister then pause to con-

sider taking their own lives. Our *sheep* and other ministers become caught in a mental fog that diminishes their absolute faith in God—their certainty that God never leaves us or forsakes us—that He will work ALL things together for our good and will carry us when we stumble and fall.

And Satan's deceptions continue into church and cultural systems that firmly believe suicide is "the unpardonable sin leading to straight to hell" denying those victims funeral/memorial services. This, in turn, touches multitudes of others who suffer the abuse of depression. This is where we must make it clear that Jesus, Himself, told us what the "unpardonable sin" is when He spoke to a large crowd saying, *"And everyone who speaks a word against the Son of Man will be forgiven, but anyone who blasphemes against the Holy Spirit will not be forgiven."* (Luke 12:10). Indeed, any blaspheme against the Holy Spirit is the ultimate sin of rejection—rejection of the Lord, Jesus, and His salvation of our souls.

So it is, that we must prayerfully reach deep into the Compassion of our Lord as we walk beside our brothers and sisters in ministry who are fighting this battle. And should our efforts fail, we must stand on the absolute Truth that God's Grace and Mercy is BIGGER than the sin of suicide and can be forgiven.

Every person who God has called to spread His Word must put aside pride, jealousy, doubt and mistrust, seek His counsel first and, if needed, seek the counsel of one of His children who is called to help us reach the point of healing. There is strength in the unity of our calling, and the Lord will always be with us as He leads us to the counselor He has selected so that "iron to sharpen iron." When our personal "iron" is dulled, rusted and broken, it needs sharpening. (Proverbs 27:17)

"For we do not wrestle against flesh and blood, but against principalities,
against powers, against the rulers of the darkness of this age,
against spiritual hosts of wickedness in the heavenly places."

Ephesians 6:12 (NKJV)

If we believe with all our hearts that Jesus Christ has saved us and that we have eternal life through His death, burial and resurrection; and we have seen Him work His miracles and save souls through our lives; why can we not receive healing for our own heart, mind and spirit? Do we not have faith for own healing but only faith for the deliverance of others? We must forgive ourselves and others, be healed, and be restored to full unity with our ministry teams, so that the sheep; those who we are called to serve and nurture—will not be scattered.

We *know* (at least intellectually) that there is truly an invisible war going on all around us every day. Simply stated, it is the battle between the Kingdom of God and the kingdom of darkness which is run by Satan, Lucifer, the fallen angel from heaven. Some may have difficulty accepting this truth. However, whether we believe it or not, it remains true. The entire Bible from Genesis to Revelations speaks of this *war of the worlds*. And the end of the book tells us quite clearly that the war is ultimately and eternally won by God, the Creator of heaven and earth!

**To be effective and victorious in THIS war,
we must have the Lord Jesus Christ living in our hearts
and be totally "sold out" to His Kingdom Plan.
By the power of His Spirit living within us,
we learn how to wage war against Satan and his tactics
and BE Victorious!**

~ ~ ~

There is one biblical story in particular that has strengthened my personal resolve to be the servant of God He has always purposed for me. It describes a conversation between God and Satan that speaks to the importance of each and every person on the planet. It is the story of Job, an individual that God calls, "My servant."

"Now there was a day when the sons of God came to present themselves before the LORD, and Satan also came among them. The LORD said to Satan, 'From where do you come?' Then Satan answered the LORD and said, 'From roaming about on the earth and walking around on it.' The LORD said to Satan, 'Have you considered My servant, Job? For there is no one like him on the earth, a blameless and upright man, fearing God and turning away from evil.'"

Job 1:6-8 (NASB)

My point here is that God has called all of us to be "blameless and upright" ministers of His Word to people everywhere. God knows everything about us and does not want us to define the terms "blameless and upright" in human, dictionary terms. His definition of those words begins and ends with Jesus—Whose shed Blood covered us and began our New lives.

There are also those who have a very specific call into Ministry which places a bigger bullseye on us—from Satan's perspective. If we have no idea how to fight this battle, we will experience defeat. Thus we must always be ready to seek God's counsel as He directs us to build His league of warriors (other ministers) for the battle.

~ ~ ~

Everyone's Personal Journey to Wholeness

Those in Ministry who have experienced the trauma of abuse have a greater mountain to climb toward wholeness. And yet, we must realize that our deeply personal journey will be used of God for His purposes and He will turn what happened (or is happening) to us—in our heart, mind, body and soul—into a most useful ministry gift.

The path we take toward recovery and wholeness is crucial to our wellbeing and the Lord leads each of us through a uniquely different process. Only He knows how intensely our peace and privacy have been disrupted, and to what degree this has affected every area of our lives. Many of us experienced such exceedingly intimate assaults that the wounds are bone-deep. Others have witnessed horrendous acts of violence, mental and emotional beatings, that we've never revealed to any other living soul—and have desperately tried to bury them deep within the crevices of our memories.

Even so, we now have the opportunity to open our hearts to God and expose our wounds to the One Who is waiting to heal us. In the process, we might be ready to share some of our painful experiences with our close relatives or friends. Unknown to us, they have been praying for the chance to support us, because the Holy Spirit has quickened in them a spirit of compassion toward us. Our willingness to first talk with God about the assaults against us, is a good sign and means that a Holy Spirit change is really happening on the inside. For this we can Praise God!

There was a time when the Apostles Paul and Barnabas were traveling together, and a few days earlier they learned that they were going to be stoned. Yet, Paul matter-of-factly said to the men they were about to commission as elders, *"We must go through many hardships to enter the kingdom of God,"* (Acts 14:22b). They were speaking to the people (soon-to-be-elders) in that room. But I believe that, through Paul, they were also speaking to every Minister who has lived through all the generations since then.

As pastors, elders, ministers, priests, we must prepare ourselves all the more diligently against the plots of Satan. Then, when we are assaulted by him and his followers, we must be willing to run to God for restoration and acknowledge that He may use the counseling gifts of one of His other children, to help us along the way. That person may not be an acknowledged counselor or even a minister. However, throughout all our lives, we must hold tight to this Promise of God:

"No weapon formed against you shall prosper,

And every tongue which rises against you in judgment
You shall condemn.
This is the heritage of the servants of the Lord,
And their righteousness is from Me,"
Says the Lord."
Isaiah 54:17 (NKJV)

Chapter 17

More About The Fight And Prevention

Throughout this book I've presented several of the Lord's Ways to combat our enemy, first and foremost being to respond to Jesus' call:

"Come to Me, all you who labor and are heavy-laden and overburdened
and I will cause you to rest.
I will ease and relieve and refresh your souls."
Matthew 11:28 (AMPC)

Now I am collecting those ideas in one place and adding a few others that pertain to the prevention of future assaults—and *protective* prevention for future generations. God has given us the Wisdom to depend on Him and know how to "be strong" as we build our defenses. It is up to us to heed His Ways.

In the Old Testament, when Joshua was given charge of the Tribes of Israel as they were about to go to war, God said to him, "*Have I not commanded you? Be strong and of good courage; do not be afraid, nor be dismayed, for the Lord your God is with you wherever you go."* (Joshua 1:9 NKJV) This is a command to us today, too, as we face spiritual battles that too often cause us physical, mental and emotional pain. If we believe God's Word, we can know beyond certainty that He is with us! And, *"if God be for us, who can be against us"* (Romans 8:31). No one, no other natural, human or spiritual entity can stand against God. He is our Shepherd who will direct our paths and lead us to safety.

Below are some of the ways God's taught us build our defenses. Each characteristic positions us in alignment with attributes of God's Own Character:

- LOVE: affection, cherish, delight, fidelity, value, regard... (The first and greatest of God's commandments—to love God above all else and to love others as He has loved us.)
- Faithful: unwavering loyalty, devoted, trustworthy, steadfast...
- Goodness: moral; virtuous, with integrity, dignity and principle...
- Grace: generosity, offering favor, support, respect, approval, acceptance...
- Holiness: obedience to God's Ways; not conforming to the world or Satan's ways...
- Jealousy: "jealously" (passionately) guarding the relationship we have with God. Example: The Apostle Paul felt a "divine jealousy" as he encouraged the Corinthians to be completely devoted to Jesus Christ (2 Corinthians 11:2).
- Justice: impartiality, fairness, ethical objectivity...
- Kindness: sympathy, tenderness, compassion, good will...

- Mercy: forgiveness, absolution, clemency, compassion...
- Patience: endurance, fortitude, persistence, diligence...
- Righteousness: honesty, integrity, morality, benevolence...
- Truthfulness: forthrightness, authenticity, sincerity, principled...
- Wisdom: insight, perception, discernment, good judgment...
- Wrath (righteous anger): 2 Corinthians 11:2 (14)

The more we allow the Holy Spirit to grow these character traits within us, the more He can build our discernment regarding the deceitful wiles of the enemy and strengthen us to defend ourselves and others.

As given in the early chapter titled Confronting the Enemy – Part One, preparing ourselves by putting on the Armor of God is vital. The LORD want's us wrapped tightly in His Truth; heart-protected in His Righteousness; walking (and talking) the Gospel message that, in turn, strengthens us with every Word; raising the Shield of Faith before us to extinguish all the attacks of the enemy; confident in our personal salvation; and wielding the Word of God with Holy Spirit Wisdom (Ephesians 6:10-11, 14-17).

Finally, the LORD expects us to cooperate with Him and grow strong enough so that we are able to protect and defend those who cannot protect themselves.

Defend the weak and the fatherless;
uphold the cause of the poor and the oppressed.
Rescue the weak and the needy;
deliver them from the hand of the wicked.
Psalm 82: 3-4 (NIV)

Statistics given earlier make it clear that we (as the society of humans on this earth) have been doing a very poor job of this—for generations. How do we correct this? Leaders around the world are debating this very question today. Yet, the only answer is to return—and/or find our way—to God, our Father/ Creator. Only when hearts are given to Him can He show the way to be aligned with His Love and Peace—and each other. 1 John 4:4 (*Ye are of God, little children, and have overcome them: because greater is He that is in you, than he that is in the world.*) Until all peoples turn to Him, we remain embroiled in human and spiritual battles, and must learn His warfare strategies, keeping ourselves as close to Him and His Principles as possible. Here are actions we can take.

- **PRAY**. Talk with God every day—about everything. If something bad is happening in your life or in someone else's life, ask Him who you should tell.
- **Submit and resist**. *"Therefore, submit to God. Resist the devil and he will flee from you."* (James 4:7)
- **Stay Alert**. Don't become complacent and return to old habits. *"You are all children of the light.... We do not belong to the night or to the darkness. So then, let us not be like others, who are asleep, but let us be awake and sober."* (1 Thessalonians 5:4-11)
- **Remember Whose Might wins the battle**: There are those who are called to the front lines, who (starting with the Jesus and the Apostles) cast out demons and throw them off cliffs. This takes much Holy Spirit preparation, and more are being called to this ministry today. *"...This is the Word of the LORD to Zerubbabel: 'Not by might nor by power, but by my Spirit,' says the LORD Almighty.* (Zechariah 4:6)
- **Be confident in your authority** to withstand the enemy. Jesus said, *"Truly I tell you, whatever you bind on*

earth will bebound in heaven, and whatever you loose on earth will beloosed in heaven." (Matthew 18:18)

· **Stand Firm** in the knowledge that Jesus has won the battle! He said, *"I have told you these things, so that in Me you may have peace. In this world you will have trouble. But take heart! I have overcome the world."* (John 16:33)

· **Believe His Promise** that the enemy cannot win! We (those who believe in Jesus) are His Church on earth. He tells us, *"...on this rock I will build my church, and the gates of hades shall not prevail against it."* (Matthew 16:18)

· **Believe His Word** that we (yes, each one of us) are conquerors in this war!

"Yet in all these things we are more than conquerors through Him who loved us.
For I am persuaded that neither death nor life,
nor angels nor principalities nor powers,
nor things present nor things to come, nor height nor depth,
nor any other created thing, shall be able to separate us from the love of God which is in Christ Jesus our Lord."
Romans 8:37-39 (NKJV)

Chapter 18

The Predator/
Perpetrator/Abuser

I would also be remiss if I did not include my current understanding of the abuser(s)—the predator(s)—we've all met in our lives. They are part of this epidemic of violence against innocent, vulnerable people. The world's solutions to slow or stop them is a challenge in every nation. One thing we do know is that these people who victimize and abuse others, were (more often than not) either abused themselves, have mental illnesses, or have sexual addictions (caused by abuse) that are twisted and violent.

The question is: If they really wanted to get help and cease their horrific behavior, where would they go to get help? My immediate answer is—to the foot of the Cross of Jesus Christ. In this chapter you'll find God's Word as well as a few pertinent statistics and some academic perspectives on this topic.

~ ~ ~

Medical doctors, social scientists, psychologists and even talk show hosts have tried to address this issue. This has been a good thing because their work brings to light the plight of victims and how to support them during their healing and restoration process. But, it has not been as successful in exposing perpetrators before their violence affects another person, or in rehabilitating them after arrest and prosecution.

So, what does the predator do when their violent acts have been uncovered and their *internal bleeding* is revealed? Medicating them does not remove their enemy, who continues to batter them with evil thoughts—but it does soothe them momentarily, as the world continues to search for solutions to resolve the problem.

Despite the academic and self-help books and programs that are now in existence for the perpetrators, they continue to die inside, often experiencing many of the same effects that the victims experience: isolation, suffocating turmoil and emotional instability. Most often, in this state of existence, the person/predator is so traumatized they have no idea how worn and damaged they are. This is a trick of the Satan to keep people in *soul-tie* bondage and spiral their actions out of control.

What I do know is that these demonic forces exist. Some of their names are: Guilt, Shame, Fear, Frustration, Anger, Hatred, and Suicide. Their goal is to push and manipulate predators to commit abusive acts, even murder, which in turn keeps them blinded to God's Love and His restoration that is available to them, too.

"...for all have sinned and fall short of the glory of God,
and all are justified freely by His grace
through the redemption that came by Christ Jesus.
God presented Christ as a sacrifice of atonement,
through the shedding of his blood—to be received by faith."
Romans 3: 23-25 (NIV)

We know that God does not show favoritism (Acts 10: 34-35). However, no matter who we are, we must all come to Him, seek His forgiveness, and believe in Him. Therefore, when these predators (abusers) are held accountable for their actions, whether through arrest and prison time or other types of confrontation (truth telling), they have the opportunity to seek Him and eventually seek the help of others. Support groups offer the chance to vent and release some of their (and our) pain, but the only real solution is the liberating Power of God. His Word, the death and resurrection of Jesus Christ, and the Power of His Spirit bring supernatural healing.

~ ~ ~

In an online article, written by John G. Taylor, (Feb. 5, 2013), I found some interesting statistics and believe it offers us some useful information. His title—*Domestic Violence and Unmasking the Terror of Dr. Jekyll and Mr. Hyde*—is quite accurate as it clearly identifies the mistreatment suffered by abuse victims and the roller coaster of confusing emotions experienced in the homes. Mr. Taylor has facilitated groups and counseled over 1,000 men who have abused their intimate partners. Here is what I learned from his "counselor" perspective.

- Domestic violence (physical, verbal, emotional and sexual abuse) is the leading cause of injury to women, sending over one million to doctor's offices or emergency rooms every year.
- This abuse occurs from the hands of the person who said, "I love you," not from the hands of strangers.
- 95% of reported domestic violence cases are men abusing women and 5% are women abusing men.
- 37% of pregnant women are battered.

Taylor also wrote about the cycle of violence that he broke into three phases: (1) Tension building, where there is a palpable tension building from or within the batterer/abuser, usually ending in an argument. (2) The explosion, when the assault happens. (3) The return to the "honeymoon phase," when the batterer/abuser apologizes for their actions and may buy the victim gifts or do something special for them in an attempt to make amends.

Mr. Taylor also includes his research on the profile of an abuser, believing that psychiatric disorders, such as borderline and antisocial personality disorders, and narcissistic personality disorder play a big role in the causes of the abuser's violent acts.

1. Jealousy (questioning the victim constantly about whereabouts, and jealous of time spent apart).
2. <u>Controlling behavior (Abusers who keep their victim from getting a job, leaving the house or even bathing without permission)</u>
3. <u>Isolation (Makes partner move away from family and friends so that they are totally dependent on them and are their only support system.)</u>
4. <u>Forced sex (Abusers who forced their partners to have sex with their friends or forces sex when their partner is asleep.)</u>
5. <u>Holds very rigid gender roles (Believes that the spouse's job is to cater to them; that they are "king/ queen of the castle.")</u>

Although Taylor sincerely believes that violent abusers can be treated successfully through group and individual therapy, he warns us that they are "very clever, smart, and extremely charming." We must all take heed to that warning and be prepared.

~ ~ ~

It has been made abundantly clear to me over many years of counseling, that these personality disorder elements are real, and need to be addressed with medical and psychiatric assistance. However, they also play into the strategies that Satan uses to deceive and manipulate abusers which, in turn, (through soul-ties) becomes their door into deceiving and manipulating their victims. **That is why it is vitally important to open ourselves up to God—Father, Son, and Holy Spirit—and seek healing. But this cannot happen until the person(s) learns Who God is.**

In Scripture we read about one occasion when Jesus was speaking with a large group, and He said: *"...If God were your Father* [if you truly knew Him as your Father], *you would love Me, for I have come here from God.... Why is my language not clear to you? Because you are unable to hear what I say. You belong to your father, the devil, and you want to carry out your father's desires. He was a murderer from the beginning, not holding to the truth, for there is no truth in him.... for he is a liar and the father of lies."* (John 8: 42-44) Yes, indeed, we have been warned against the clever lies, charming deceits and manipulations of the enemy—both human and spiritual.

~ ~ ~

I now return to the question at the beginning of this chapter: If abusers wanted to get help and cease their horrific behavior, where would they go to get the help? There is but one answer—the answer that is given to each and every one of us. We must seek God our true Father Who has loved us before we were conceived—then we must seek His healing that He's kept available to us even before we considered turning to Him.

> *For when we were still without strength, in due time Christ died for the ungodly.... God demonstrates His own love toward us, in that while we were still sinners, Christ died for us. Much more then, having now been justified by His blood, we shall be saved from wrath through Him. For if when we were enemies we were reconciled to God through the death of His Son, much more, having been reconciled, we shall be saved by His life. And not only that, but we also*

*rejoice in God through our Lord Jesus Christ, through
Whom we have now received the reconciliation.*
    Romans 5: 6-11 (NKJV)

Chapter 19

There Is Greatness Locked Up Inside Of You!

"Before I formed you in the womb, I knew you."
Jeremiah 1:5

Our individual lives (body, soul and spirit) were created by God with a uniquely designed purpose even before we were born, and He tells us that we are fearfully and wonderfully made—to give Him glory through those purposes, and to live life abundantly through His Son Jesus Christ!

"I will praise You, for I am fearfully and wonderfully made;
Marvelous are Your works, And that my soul knows very well." Psalm 139:14

I have come that they may have life and have it to the full.
John 10:10b (NIV)

This book, **Healed Am I**, is God's very personal gift to you. Yes, I was obedient to write it, and it is my very personal gift to you, too. What He has released into your hands will open many doors that you thought were permanently closed.

<u>**Healed Am I, is also a declaration that you can now make,**</u> <u>**that describes your mental, emotional and spiritual state of**</u> <u>**being; whole and complete because of what God has done in-**</u> <u>**side of your very being!**</u>

Satan's plan to steal you, steal from you, kill and destroy you has been CANCELLED!

As you've prayed the prayers in these chapters and accepted Jesus and His Unconditional Love into your heart, His Healing and Restoration process began! He meant what He said, that we are meant to have Life and have it more abundantly. It is our Creator's desire that we not just exist, but have fullness of joy, love, peace, purpose and direction for each day. No matter where we've been in life, or what we've been through, there is always Hope to begin life anew. That is just how much God loves us!

So, as you close this book, this is your opportunity to begin again on that path of Hope and great expectation for your future! Now you will see things from a healthier perspective, God's perspective, not through an emotional window of pain and sorrow.

However, some may be experiencing similar aftermath days like I did. I realized that after speaking the truth of what happened to me, forgiving the abusers, praying and reading the Word, there was still a numbness in my soul. I could not really *feel*. There was a fear of trusting and loving again. So, you know what God did? He showed me an open vision of His Hand reaching in and removing my beaten, torn and worn-out heart and replacing it with a new one. I shared this experience with you in the *Healed in Relationships* chapter and share it again, now, because that moment continues to bless me in this very day and hour. He gave me a brand-new heart! And that is what He is doing for you, too.

This is, of course, received by Faith. It is a sealing and healing of our souls. God gives us a second chance at living a life of joy, peace and happiness; something we thought would never be attainable for us for the rest of our lives. But GOD, shows us each day just how wrong we were. Our life perspectives will become clearer. We will breathe easier, no longer filled with fear, because of the freedom He's given us within our spirits!

We've finally come to understand that our abuse, however dark and painful,
does not define who we are as a person!
The act(s) of violence against us does not belong to us!
Breathe in that truth right now.
Exhale the old memories and breathe in more of the Truth of who you are!

~ ~ ~

For most of my life, there has been an event in Jesus' ministry that touched me profoundly. It speaks to the Faith that one woman acted upon to receive her healing—and speaks to the Faith that I now claim, and I believe you do too. It is the story of the woman with the *issue of blood* who seized her opportunity to be healed—and the moment is conveyed to us by three of the apostles: Matthew 9:20-24; Mark 5:25-34; Luke 8:43-48.

"*When she heard about Jesus, she came up behind him in the crowd*
and touched his cloak, because she thought,
'If I just touch his clothes, I will be healed.'"
Mark 5: 27-28 (NIV)

This woman *knew*, and believed in her heart, that Jesus held the power to heal her even before she touched Him. She *knew* that her healing was going to take place. This is the essence of faith. She came from behind Him and reached for Him. And that, my friends, is exactly what we must do! Reach for Jesus and receive what we need from the Him, every day. He has an endless supply of healing and health for us!

But Jesus kept looking around to see who had done it.

*Then the woman, knowing what had happened to her,
came and fell at his feet and, trembling with fear
told him the whole truth.
He said to her, 'Daughter, your faith has healed you.
Go in peace and be freed from your suffering.'"*
Mark 5: 32-34 (NIV)

Jesus did not pursue her, specifically, other than speaking Truth everywhere He went. His message came to her ears, and she *believed*, creating this deliberate and determined act of Faith within her.

We are not given information about what the exact medical problem was, but we know it caused her to bleed continuously for 12 years. (In biblical numerology the number 12 represents order.) We also know that she'd received various treatments from various "physicians" who only made things worse. After those many years of suffering "cures" at the hands of men, we can well imagine her physical weakness and the fear and depression that caused her much *internal bleeding* as well. The culture she lived in would have shunned her, and people would yell out "unclean" every time they even caught a glimpse of her. Yet her humiliation and distress finally came to an end when she heard that Jesus would be coming through her neighborhood. And when she touched the hem of His garment her bleeding stopped immediately! After 12 achingly long years her body, heart and mind and spirit were once again put in order.

Your suffering may have been for 12 years or more, *bleeding internally* from mental, emotional and spiritual damage done by physical abuse. I believe that we are not given this woman's name so that we can all imagine ourselves as this tormented, then healed person (man, woman or child), healed and restored through Jesus Christ.

So, let's take a moment and imagine. In your mind's eye, place yourself in that big crowd with people jostling to get closer; get a better look at this man called Jesus. Yes, He's there, and you see His shoulders as the crowd parts just enough so you might get a little closer. You wrap your shawl tighter around your head and face so people won't recognize you and realize that the only way you'll ever get next to Him is if you get on your hands and knees and move forward—like the children are doing.

<u>Jesus is walking slowly because the crowd is so dense. You see His sandals, then reach out and touch the hem of His garment. This is your act of faith!</u>

"At once Jesus realized that power had gone out from Him. He turned around in the crowd and asked, "Who touched my clothes?" Mark 5:30

We do not have to imagine the Power of Jesus Christ touching us! With our act of Faith, believing in Him and reaching out for Him, His power to give us new life will pour into us (into you) immediately! He will give you wholeness from every "issue" of torment you've ever experienced.

There is a beautifully intricate connection between receiving and believing. If we heard that someone we didn't know wanted to give us a gift, we would hesitate to accept it (especially in these days of package bombs). However, when we learn that someone who loves us wants to give us a gift, we're ready to receive it, because we have faith in them and trust that the gift is a good thing.

This anonymous woman who was healed had *heard* of Jesus and the power He'd used to heal others of all kinds of diseases—and she *believed* that He was Who He said He was, the Son of God. She *believed* that the demonstrations of His power were not magic, or psychic phenomena, but the Supernatural Power of God!

"Jesus answered, "I did tell you, but you do not believe. The works I do in my Father's name testify about me, ...
I give them eternal life, and they shall never perish;

...I and the Father are one."
John 10: 25-30
Her belief...gave her Faith...to receive her healing!

~ ~ ~

I hope and pray that you, too, **believe** and have discovered your personal Faith in God (Father, Son, and Holy Spirit), and have received your healing. However, there may be a few readers who have had a really tough time reading through this book, or even reading segments of it, because they don't believe that God even exists. The enemy has trapped them in a spiraling loop that keeps them focused on churches that were not responsive to their needs, or people who call themselves Christians yet lie, cheat, steal and abuse others. They see others in happy and healthy relationships with friends and loved ones and are certain they can never attain the same. The enemy has stolen their hope and dreams, churning up memories that bring them constant *internal bleeding.*

To these readers I must speak Truth. **I can tell you with absolute certainty that God is as real as the air you are breathing.** His Love for you is SO BIG that it is unfathomable! He showed this Great Love to you by sending His Son, Jesus Christ, into this world where He was tortured, crucified and died, to once and for all time atone for your sins and reconcile you to Himself, even while you sit there today in unbelief. And He awaits your decision. Will you accept the free gift of salvation He offers to you? The benefits package is the best you will ever receive.

"For God so loved the world
that He gave His one and only Son
that whoever believes in Him
shall not perish but have eternal life."
John 3:16 (NIV)

I have counseled precious people who have been so physically and mentally battered and bruised that they had become numb and had no real sense of what a normal or healthy life is supposed to look like and were having a difficult time believing in God at any level. They knew that their situation was unhealthy and destructive, but they learned to live with the pain, block out the surface memories and they saw no way of escape. They were *just surviving* with no hope of escaping the torment where depression and low self-esteem were literally choking the life out of them. As I told them what God had done for me, they found it almost too good to be true and yet it is!

"Jesus said to him, 'I am the Way, and the Truth, and the Life;

no one comes to the Father but through Me.'"

John 14:6

"Behold, I stand at the door and knock.

*If **anyone** hears My voice and opens the door,*

I will come in to him and dine with him, and he with Me."

Revelation 3:20

Yes! When we "open the door" and let Him in, the Lord, Jesus, comes into our lives and "dines with us." With the greatest Love, He walks with us, teaches us, guides us, Shepherd's us, and sets us free—free beyond our wildest imaginations! We begin to learn, grow and mature with Him, preparing for an Eternal Life of Love and Joy in His Presence.

Jesus knocks at your door today. Will you open it?

The following prayer...

...is but one conversation people have with God when they accept His gift. **Whatever way you choose to phrase your words when talking with Him, will be perfect.** He sees your heart and totally understands.

Hello God. You may not recognize my voice, at least in this tone, because when I've called out to You I was usually cursing You for allowing bad things to happen to me. But today, I've come to believe that You really do love me and have loved me

since before I was born. Thank You for sending Your
Son, Jesus, to die for me. I'm so sorry for all the sins
I've committed, many of them blamed on You and
the evil person who abused me. I ask Your forgiveness for all that I've done that hurt You, and I accept Jesus as my personal Savior. With this Faith, I
put my trust in You, God, and look forward to living
in the Ways You will teach me. Amen.

~ ~ ~

Praise God! I am so excited for you! Now your relationship
with God will grow and your relationships with others will
become healthy and gratifying. When God restores us, it is
complete. There is nothing missing, nothing lacking, and nothing broken! You may notice that people will start seeing your
transformation. You are not the same person, because God
has brought liberty and freedom to your soul, mind and spirit!
God's peace now rests upon you and it will be evident in every
facet of your life.

Then finally, there comes a moment in time when you *know*
that you have real peace! The pain from your memories of
abuse are gone, the misery has ended, and your heart is free
and healed. Your mind is at rest. There is nothing between your
soul and your God! You are His beloved child! You can breathe
again; really breathe freely in and out. There is no evidence of
your pain and the past is only noticed by a few scars. Your *internal bleeding* and *mourning* has stopped! Every root of the
enemy's soul-ties has been ripped out! Your healing is complete! Your spirit is quiet and at rest. This is the peace that only
God can give.

Now live!
Live your life to the fullest! The best is yet to come!

Chapter 20

Points To Ponder

To encourage you, my friends, as you walk forward, I believe it is important to summarize the core elements of this book and offer you several definitions that have helped me, too.

- **The LORD our God is no respecter of persons!** What God has done for me and for many others I know—He is more than able to do for you.
  Then Peter opened his mouth and said:
  "In truth I perceive that God shows no partiality."
  Acts 10:34
- **We would be wise** to learn about the strategies of the enemy – yet never fear them.
  The thief does not come except to steal, and to kill, and to destroy.
  I have come that they may have life, and that they may have it more abundantly.
  John 10:10
  [Jesus said] *These things I have spoken to you, that in Me you may have peace.*
  In the world you will have tribulation; but be of good

cheer,
I have overcome the world.
John 16:33

- **Face the reality** of the pain—the *internal bleeding* and the *mourning* for the things that could have been different. Uncover it and seek freedom for your soul and spirit. Psalm 32 is one of King David's "contemplations." One particular sentence (vs. 3) catches my attention every time I read it:
When I kept silent, my bones grew old , through my groaning all the day long.
David was specifically talking about the need to confess the wrongs we've done in our lives—and we can all benefit from do that. However, this also relates to keeping silent about what has happened to us through no fault of our own. The same enemy that deceived David into committing adultery and murder, is the same enemy who deceived our abusers to assault us—and the same enemy who has deceived us into believing the truth is better kept secret, so he can continue to use it against us.

- **Give yourself the gift of introspection**. Take a moment now and write down the feelings, thoughts or prayers that are on your heart. Describe how freedom feels to you and how it will change the way you live, breathe and relate to others from this moment forward.
"Be still, and know that I am God;"
Psalm 46a

- **Remembering/Revealing/Releasing**. You took a bold step to revisit and remember the place and time when your abuse took place. You then uncovered or revealed that pain through talking with God about it and even revealing it to others. Most importantly, you have released your pain to God and forgiven the perpetrator(s) which, in turn, secures your own freedom and peace of mind.

· **Forgiving Is Divine**. Our ability to forgive those who abused us comes only from God.
"Then Peter came to Jesus and asked,
'Lord, how many times shall I forgive my brother
or sister who sins against me? Up to seven times?'
Jesus answered, "I tell you, not seven times, but seventy-seven times."
Matthew 18: 21-22 (NIV)

· **Never Forget Jesus' Words of Healing**.
"Then He said to her, 'Daughter, your faith has healed you. Go in peace.'"
Luke 8:48

This is a command, a charge from the Lord to proceed forward from this place with peace ruling and reigning in your future. Truly, your future is bright!

· **Never Forget God's Promises for your future.**
"For I know the plans I have for you," declares the Lord,
"plans to prosper you and not to harm you, plans to give
you hope and a future."
Jeremiah 29:11

· **God's Perfect Timing.** Occasionally, I still hear the whisper from the enemy tempting me to become angry with God—again. That's when I reread the Scripture about the man who had been an invalid for 38 years. BUT GOD sent His Son, Jesus, and suddenly the man was healed. One of our divinely designed purposes is to give God the Glory, and our moments of healing do, indeed, do that...to the world! Especially as we walk forward with Him!
"Then Jesus said to him, 'Get up! Pick up your mat and

walk.'
At once the man was cured; he picked up his mat and
walked."
John 5:8

- **Salvation is God's Gift!** God demonstrates His own love for us in this: *While we were still sinners, Christ died for us.* Now that your healing has begun, it is clear that God has been there all along. His love for you is greater than all of the pain from the past! It is liberating and restorative. From this day forward, you are free to enjoy all of the benefits of this Great Salvation through Jesus Christ, the Son of the Living God!

- **Uprooting the Root.** The demonic root of abuse, torment, shame, rejection, sadness, depression, and bipolar symptoms are destroyed by and through God's Power, leaving His healing and wholeness.

- **Destroy the Fruit.** With the evil root now being uprooted, the poisoned fruit can no longer be reproduced. For the first time in a long time you are truly free. Pain, depression, turmoil, torment, sadness, low self-esteem, bitterness, rejection and fear are gone! You are cleansed and restored by the healing power of God through Jesus Christ. God has answered each prayer as you have prayed while reading these pages.

- **Pain Free.** *The chastisement of our peace was upon Him and by His stripes were healed.* (Isaiah 53:5) The death, burial and resurrection of Jesus Christ is Finished Work! Our complete healing was paid for by His sacrifice over 2,000 years ago.

- **Peace with God.** *Thou wilt keep him in perfect peace whose mind is stayed on thee...* (Isaiah 26:3) There is nothing more valuable and life-changing than peace

with God. It surpasses having all of the earthly posses-
sions you could dream of. Peace is Priceless!!!
- **Wholeness:**
    - Nothing missing
    - Nothing Broken
    - Nothing Lacking
- **SHALOM.** This word is a Hebrew word meaning peace.
In true context its meaning goes much deeper.
"Shalom" is taken from the root word *shalom*, which
means, "to be safe in mind, body, or estate." It speaks
of completeness, fullness, or a type of wholeness that
encourages you to give back — to generously re-pay
something in some way. When you greet someone or
say goodbye, you say, Shalom. You are literally saying,
"may you be full of well-being" or, "may health and
prosperity be upon you." (firm.org.il, 2018)
- **NEW LIFE.** *If any man be in Christ He is a new crea-
ture, old things are passed away and behold all things
become new.* 2 Corinthians 5:17

Look at this list as your personal checklist as you journey
through your healing process. From time to time, go back to
it to be sure that you are free and affirm your freedom! There
may come a time when you can share your process with others
to help them begin their own healing journey.

Chapter 21

Dear Reader

If you believe that someone you know is being abused, physically, sexually, or otherwise, reach out to them. Let them know that you are concerned. Give them an opportunity to talk with you and share. If they do, please give them the rescue hotline numbers listed below (or local numbers that you've found) or place this book in their hands and encourage them to read it.

The National Domestic Violence Hotline **1-800-799-7233**
…or **1-855-812-1011 for deaf or hard of hearing.**
National Suicide Prevention Lifeline **1-800-273-8255**
Child Help National Abuse Hotline **1-800-422-4453**

And if you, personally, have been blessed through the reading of these pages I would love to hear from you! Please write to me and share your testimony. Let what God does in your life continue to bless others.

Peace and Blessings,

Beverly Tipton Hammond, Pure Water Ministries
facebook.com/Pure Water Ministries International
tiptonhammond@yahoo.com

References Reviewed

Understanding PTSD: www.webmd.com

U.S. Bureau of Justice Statistics. 2000 Sexual Assault of Young Children as Reported to Law Enforcement. 2000, PDF report by Dr. Howard N. Snyder

www.childhelp.org, (2012)

Letourneau University, 2012, Article, "Confronting an Abuser" by Justin and Lindsey Holcomb: www.mentorguide.familylife.com (confronting-an-abuser)

National Institute of Justice & Centers for Disease Control & Prevention. Prevalence, Incidence and Consequences of Violence Against Women Survey. 1998.

U.S. Department of Justice. 2003 National Crime Victimization Survey, 2003.

U.S. Bureau of Justice Statistics, Sex Offenses and Offenders, 1997.

1998, Commonwealth Fund Survey of the Health of Adolescent Girls, 1998.

U.S. Department of Health & Human Services, Administration for Children and Families. 1995 Child Maltreatment Survey. 1995.

Child Help, www.childhelp.org

U.S. Bureau of Justice Statistics. American Indians and Crime, 1992-2002.

World Health Organization, 2002.

U.S. Department of Justice, 2012 National Crime Victimization Survey, 2012.

Fellowship of Israel Related Ministries, www.firm.org

CPSIA information can be obtained
at www.ICGtesting.com
Printed in the USA
LVHW110955260522
719840LV00009B/43

9 780578 607023